retail design

academia

= AN AVA BOOK

Published by AVA Publishing SA
Rue des Fontenailles 16
Case Postale
1000 Lausanne 6
Switzerland
T +41 786 005 109
E enquiries@avabooks.ch

Distributed by Thames & Hudson (ex-North America)
181a High Holborn
London WC1V 7QX
United Kingdom
T +44 20 7845 5000
F +44 20 7845 5055
E sales@thameshudson.co.uk
www.thamesandhudson.com

Distributed in the USA and Canada by
Ingram Publisher Services Inc.
1 Ingram Blvd.
La Vergne TN 37086
USA
T +1 866 400 5351
F +1 800 838 1149
E customer.service@ingrampublisherservices.com

English Language Support Office
AVA Publishing (UK) Ltd.
T +44 1903 204 455
E enquiries@avabooks.ch

Copyright © AVA Publishing SA 2010

ISBN 978-2-940411-22-1

10 9 8 7 6 5 4 3 2 1

Design by
Dechant Grafische Arbeiten, Vienna

Production by AVA Book Production Pte. Ltd., Singapore
T +65 6334 8173
F +65 6259 9830
E production@avabooks.com.sg

= **TOPSHOP**
New York, USA

DESIGNER
= **DALZIEL AND POW**

DATE
= **2009**

Introduction

The aim of this book is to examine the processes and strategies of designing space for retail.

Shopping is an activity that is part of our everyday lives. Whether we are shopping to feed ourselves, clothe ourselves or simply out of enjoyment, the places we choose to shop say something about our lifestyle, culture and interests. We create a relationship with the retail environment we feel comfortable with and reject spaces that do not match our image.

The design of shops is an ever-changing cycle, following fashion trends and consumer aspirations. Retail spaces are at the forefront of contemporary interior design because they are updated regularly to stay competitive and appealing. Some of the most innovative and interactive interiors can be seen in the retail sector.

Designing retail interiors is complex, beginning with the analysis of a brand and identity. The aim of the designer is to entice, excite and enthral the consumer by creating an experience to which they can relate.

This book thoroughly guides you through each step of the retail design process, providing strategies that can produce a successful retail space and a design that is appropriate for the brand, product, consumer and retailer. This will be seen through images and drawings from practice, as well as student project work.

= **CLUB 21,**
EMPORIO ARMANI

DESIGNER
= **FOUR IV**

DATE
= **2006**

Designing space for retail is a complex and ever-changing process. It is hoped that this book will take the reader on a journey through the retail space, exploring the strategies and relationships to be found at each step of the way.

How to get the most out of this book

This book introduces different aspects of
retail design, via dedicated chapters for
each topic. Using a variety of examples
from both students and professionals,
the processes and strategies involved in
designing space for retail are examined,
analysed and debated.

SECTION HEADERS
Current section headings are clearly named in
the navigation bar. The numbers of topics
within the chapter are indicated by vertical
dividers. Past and future section headings are
displayed above the navigation bar.

\ Home \

Retail sectors Leisure and entertainment

054/055

= **REEBOK FLASH
STORE**
New York, USA

DESIGNER
= **FORMAVISION**

DATE
= **2002**

Recently, Reebok
re-invented itself in a
new consumer offer.
The Reebok Flash Store
opened in New York for
a limited period in the
CV2 Contemporary Art
Gallery, selling retro and
limited edition footwear.
Formavision, whose
trademark is to use art
as part of their interior
scheme, designed the
space.

**The leisure and entertainment
sector has grown significantly in
the last ten years. Whether the
activity is based around a destination
or a product purchase, the chances
are the interior space will encapsulate
a brand. An outing to the cinema,
museum or theatre will each give an
opportunity to buy into the experience
through a shop, bar or café.**

The leisure sector includes sport – as an
activity or apparel; technology – sound,
audio and gaming; travel – modes of
transport and travel agency; and finance –
the services of banks and building societies.
Banks are now abandoning the high street
and going online.

Sport

In recent years, the sports industry
has taken on the idea of enforcing their
global brand identity through store
image. Retail spaces within the sports
sector are sparse in products and are
exhibition-like in the way that the
participator moves around the space
and interacts with displays. The graphic
language is prominent throughout and
a theme demonstrating youth and
physicality encapsulates the brand
message.

Sports brand Nike has opened a series
of Nike Towns around the world, each
Town taking its interior influence from
the surrounding city. In 2002, Reebok
also opened its world headquarters in
Boston, USA. The Reebok brand is
encapsulated in its headquarters and is
reinforced in every aspect of Reebok
design – from the apparel to the shop
floor – on every high street.

FORM AND FUNCTION
Interior designers and architects differ widely in
their views of how far the function of a space
should affect its design. Form and function are
discussed in greater detail in the AVA title, Basics
Interior Architecture: Form + Structure.

SECTION INTRODUCTIONS
Each section is introduced by a
few brief paragraphs.

THINKING POINTS
Key design concepts
and some of the debate
surrounding them.

CAPTIONS
Detailed captions give information on the specifics of each project and the thinking behind the design decisions taken.

RUNNING GLOSSARY
Key terms are explained clearly and precisely within their context.

PULL QUOTES
Thoughts from well-known designers and retail experts provide insight into the world of retail design.

STUDENT CASE STUDIES
Examples of student work enable the reader to see how theory is put into practice.

QUESTIONS AND EXERCISES
Questions in summary allow the reader to consider how they might approach a design project.

Branding is an approach used to market products and services under a particular name. We can all identify with brands that are familiar to us and part of our everyday life. But how does a brand translate from two dimensions into the volume of an interior space? The answer is somewhat complex and forms the basis of the design process; understanding a brand is one of the most important aspects of the retail designer's role. In most interior design, understanding a building is the starting point and subject of investigation. In retail, however, the brand is the starting point and the building or site often comes later.

THIS CHAPTER **explores the notion of branding and examines how branding principles can be interpreted into an interior scheme. Different mechanisms for defining a brand are set out and examples of retail types are showcased to explain ways of appealing to consumer markets and trends through the interior.**

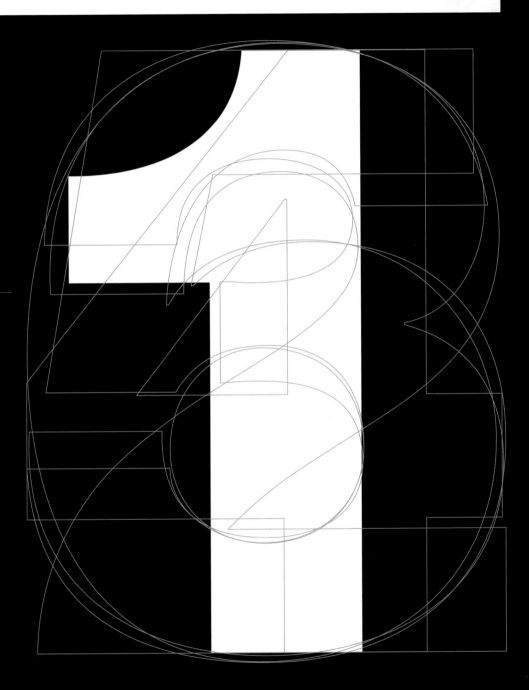

Branding and identity   What is branding?

The concept of branding is intrinsically linked with advertising, marketing and playing on the subconscious aspirations of the consumer. A brand can be a product, a person or a logo – anything that can be bought and sold, as an idea or artefact, can be branded.

Branding is a global culture fuelled by consumerism and the need for people to categorise their lifestyles, likes and dislikes through buying into particular products. It is evident that brands possess values that distinguish them from their competitors. It is interesting to consider why we buy a branded product over a supermarket named equivalent at half the price. What makes us believe that the contents of the tin are of a better quality?

Some brands have crossed boundaries in becoming the name associated with the product. For instance, an MP3 player is most commonly called an iPod, at a bar we ask for coke (Coca Cola) rather than Pepsi. The power of the brand is evident in our everyday lives and our language is cluttered with brand references.

No brand can appeal to everyone. Through marketing and advertising, the image of the brand is identified and sold to the public. The brand can be defined by analysing its core values through understanding the product, communicating it to the right consumer audience and understanding that audience, and finally matching the product to the physical environment.

In retail terms, the store is built around the concept of the brand and the products sold within it. The interior emulates the aspirations of the brand values and qualities to enhance the relationship between the space and the message. Everything about the brand must be consistent – from the associated colour and graphic style to the product range, whether diverse or focused, and the interior. This consistency makes the message stronger and re-affirms the brand's worth.

= **PRIMARK FLAGSHIP STORE**
London, UK

DESIGNER
= **DALZIEL AND POW**

DATE
= **2007**

Primark has seen a continuing success in the UK and is true to its brand values: fast fashion and lean operations. The flagship store in London makes a bold interior statement, creating a strong presence. This scheme is the basis from which future stores will be rolled out, both in the UK and throughout Europe. Dalziel and Pow's involvement in every aspect of the Primark brand, from corporate identity and sub-brand strategies, through to the store environment and its graphic treatments, has ensured a strong, consistent identity across its stores.

Branding and identity   What is branding?

= **TIMES
SQUARE
New York, USA**

Competing
brands vie for
attention in
New York's
Times Square.

Evolution of branding

The earliest examples of branding can be
traced back as far as the 1880s when logos
began to appear on food packages such
as Campbell's soup, Coca Cola and Lyle's
Golden Syrup. The use of branding began
as a catch-phrase or image attached to a
product. It wasn't until the late 1940s that
organisations began to adjust the laws of
advertising to describe their business and
function, rather than products, and the term
'brand identity' became mainstream in
corporate language.

The concept of branding really took off in
the 1980s, following the recession and
the downturn in profits and productivity of
some of the world's largest manufacturers.
For the first time, production could be
moved overseas, to places such as China
and India, for a fraction of the cost, due
to a reform in the law governing labour
and trade. Prior to this, masterminding
the manufacturing process was the core
business strategy; this slowly began to be
replaced by developing the brand essence.

In the 1990s, big-brand names favoured
cutting the prices of their products to
spending money on advertising due to
the market downturn, with detrimental
consequences. Many did not survive the
aftermath of the recession and Wall Street
predicted the 'death of the brand'. Those
who stayed true to their brand values and
marketing strategy did survive and are still
major players in the retail sector today.

Principles of branding

Every brand image is formed by defining the main principles behind its meaning. As well as considering the product and its environment, it is important to maintain a vision of how to establish a brand and how it stands alongside its competitors. As already discussed, those brands that stay true to their brand values are able to survive and conquer in a ferociously competitive world. For example, is the brand a market leader or follower? Does the brand aspire to stand alone or does it welcome the influx of other brands? Does the brand have a wide or narrow focus in terms of product diversity? Is the brand global or local? Does the brand have longevity or is it frequently changed? These principles begin to question and inform the organisation's mission statement and are at the core of the brand's strategy.

: **PHIL KNIGHT, NIKE**
Nike is 'a sports company'; its mission is not to sell shoes but to 'enhance people's lives through sports and fitness' and to keep 'the magic of sports alive'.

The principles of a brand can be examined under the following headings:

Essence The essence identifies what is at the heart of the business and the nature of the work. These are the most important features of the organisation.

Values The term 'brand values' can be explored through what the organisation's morals and standards are and how they manifest themselves in the brand.

Image The brand image is one of the most important aspects of brand development and is paramount in showing the essence and values of the organisation to the world through visual means.

Big ideas The big ideas demonstrate what the brand sets out to achieve.

Cash generator Behind every brand is the ambition to make money. It is fundamental to know how this will happen.

Strange attractor The success of many brands is in the unknown and the additional offers that can be made under a brand. It is important to question what else people use/need the brand for.

Culture Who is the market/consumer/user and what does it feel like to be part of this culture?

Branding and identity   What is branding?

: **WALLY OLINS**
... to be really effective you have to
be able to sense the brand. You may
even be able to touch it and feel it.
So that it manifests the core idea.

= **SPORTSGIRL STORE**
Melbourne, Australia

DESIGNER
= **HMKM**

DATE
= **2008**

Sportsgirl is a well-known Australian brand.
This store in Melbourne encapsulates
the ethos of the brand through its funky
displays, graphics and interactive features
and is an exciting reinvention for this
fashion high-street retailer. A diamond-
mirrored fascia leads through to an 'urban
chic' warehouse-style space with exposed
brick and matt grey flooring and a blank
canvas area, designed to showcase
new trends and designs. More elaborate
areas such as the shoe and accessory
department, which features a floor-to-
ceiling chest of drawers, and the 'Butterfly
Garden' fitting rooms, combine to create
an energetic and colourful space, reflective
of the youthful Sportsgirl brand.

Branding and identity Developing a brand

In order to develop or reinvent a brand, the organisation involved will go through a series of processes to gain an understanding of the brand's nature or, in the case of reinvention, to consider what is not working.

Organisations often employ brand consultants to manage this process, as they may not have the expertise in-house. There are various stages involved. The first stage is to conduct research and analysis to investigate the nature of the organisation and its characteristics. This is done through auditing the organisation's existing position in terms of retail space, products or facilities, for example. Also at this point, the organisation may look to examine its main competitors in order to define their place in the market. The information generated during this initial stage then goes on to inform the development of the brand and to create a core idea from which everything about the organisation can be derived.

The next stage sees the involvement of graphic designers as they contextualise the meanings behind the core ideas, questioning how the brand looks and feels. This would be demonstrated through graphic mood and lifestyle boards as a starting point. Once the feel and look is established and agreed between designer and client, a style can be established that will work for both the graphic and interior design. This is a good example of how graphic designers and interior designers work together. Sometimes this process includes the development of a new name or logo, or working with a style that already exists. During the graphic design process, all kinds of decisions are made as to how the brand will appear in advertising. Once the designs have been agreed, the brand guidelines are established in a manual that is put together by the graphic designer. The guidelines are an important document that is given to all contractors involved in advertising and signage so that consistency is kept throughout the implementation stage. The guidelines include logo information, colour references, typeface and imagery, as well as examples of how to set out different types of signage, stationery and other communication tools. This manual also informs the graphic quality and finishes for the interior spaces.

Branding the interior

Imagine a shell of a building that is a blank canvas with neutral walls, floors and ceilings. Think of a well-known brand and the associated colour, pattern, logo, sound or scent. Understand the product and who might buy it. Analyse the lifestyle of someone who would use this brand: What car do they drive? Where do they live? How much money do they earn? And most importantly, what would they expect from a retail experience? All of these questions form the basis from which to develop a concept that will underpin the interior scheme. The term used for turning a brand into a three-dimensional spatial experience is 'brandscaping'.

Developing an interior concept

The interior scheme often takes its lead from the graphic guidelines, through understanding the aspirations of the end-user and through analysing the competition. This information is portrayed through visual research or 'mood boards' (images and photographs retrieved from books or journals that explain clearly the thought process and ideas of the design team) but will be interior orientated rather than graphically based. The key features of the visual research are then extracted into 'stories' that lead to explicit ideas about what the interior design scheme could be and how the graphic identity would impact on the space. From this process, an interior concept is born.

: OTTO RIEWOLDT
Brandscaping transforms the brand itself into a location.

Brandscaping
This is a term used to describe the mapping of a brand in a three-dimensional space.

Branding and identity   Developing a brand

Concept interpretation

The concept is then interpreted into a 'mock' interior space through visual storyboards that may contain adjacency and circulation plans, animated sketch visuals and samples of material finish. It is common for different schemes to emerge at this time, all of which will be presented to the client. The client and designer then work together to come to a conclusive design idea: this may result clearly from just one of the presented concepts or may result from a combination of all the potential concepts. Once the concept has been decided, the designer then works on the detail of the design. This process builds with each client meeting until a conclusion is reached and a set of drawings can be produced in the form of a manual.

'Rolling out' a scheme

Once a design concept has been agreed between client and designer, a programme begins to 'roll out' the new interior into the client's existing or new sites. The term 'roll out' simply means to reproduce the same interior across different sites. In order for this to happen, the manual prepared by the design team must contain all of the elements of the design, describing ways to adapt the scheme for different types of site. A variety of layouts and elevational configurations are drawn up, as well as detailed drawings for every fixture and fitting, a finishes schedule and lighting information.

Sometimes the designer's role ends there and the information is handed over to the client, who in turn employs a contractor to oversee and implement the design in each store. On other occasions, the designer will work with the client and contractors to prepare separate drawing packages for each site, using the manual as a guide for consistency. This would entail dealing with local authority planning departments and making site visits. This would usually be at the start of a project, midway through the programme, and to 'snag' the site, fixing final details, before handover at the end of the build. The designer would also liase with the contractor regarding any queries that may arise. The designer may also become involved with the visual merchandising of the store, although most large retailers have their own in-house team specifically tasked with dressing every store the same.

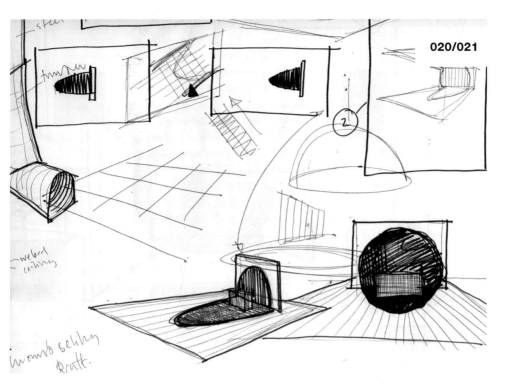

= **FULLCIRCLE FLAGSHIP STORE**
London, UK

DATE
= **2008**

The design for this flagship store is a
literal interpretation of the Fullcircle
brand. A 'floating' white, architectural
box, set within the envelope of the
original landlord's space, has been cut
away to reveal a dramatic optical illusion
that, when viewed from the shop
entrance, describes a 12-metre-wide
full circle at the rear of the store.
The images shown here demonstrate
the development of the design scheme,
from sketch to final execution.

Branding and identity Developing a brand

Building the interior

The design of a branded interior is often split into clear areas of development in each site. The analysis of this reveals some surprising results. Approximately 70 per cent of the client's budget would be spent on the architecture of the building, meaning repair or structural alteration work, electrics and services as well as flooring, ceilings and lighting. These elements are critical to the interior structure but would not necessarily be apparent to the customer. They must, however, have the potential to last up to 20 years, so are a worthwhile outlay for the client.

Secondly, the fixtures and fittings to display the merchandise and make the store function would cost approximately 20 per cent of the client's budget and would have a lifespan of around six years. Although they are important in terms of function and fit within the design of the overall scheme, the customer would not necessarily notice them.

The final 10 per cent of the budget pays for the branded elements of the scheme, through graphic communication, finish (colour, pattern or texture for instance), logos displayed where possible, music or scent. This is the critical element that finally dresses the space and portrays the lifestyle of the brand. These elements may be changed every season, week or day if fashion and trend demands it and they mimic the key message of the moment. The retail store is under constant reinvention.

: **RASSHIED DIN**
The retail designer's task is to combine elements of psychology, technology and ergonomics with the retailer's knowledge of the market.

= **VERTU STORE**
London, UK

DESIGNER
= **SHED DESIGN**

DATE
= **2007**

Shed were asked to redesign Vertu's channels, from in-store concessions and point of sale. In the design for the concession in Selfridges, London, corporate black units, glazed screens and marble flooring all add to the luxurious, opulent feel of the brand. These images show the construction of a new façade and the completed shopfront once the work has been done.

Branding and identity Selling the brand

**Although brand stores can
be seen throughout the world
in different formats, there are
particular mechanisms in place
for promoting a new concept
or to consolidate a brand
experience on the global market.**

This usually happens in major retail
positions, to allow access to the larger
proportion of the world's consumers.
The design is then reinterpreted down
into the smaller stores outside of the
major cities. These mechanisms can
be categorised as concept stores,
flagship stores and lifestyle stores.
As the retail market becomes more
and more saturated, retailers are
constantly trying to find new ways
to appeal to different markets. Online
selling has become mainstream for
most. More interestingly, the approach
of guerrilla marketing has taken retailing
by storm, bringing an element of
surprise and the unexpected to
the consumer.

= **GINA CONCEPT STORE
Dubai, UAE**

DESIGNER
= **CAULDER MOORE**

DATE
= **2009**

After establishing the Gina brand in
two prominent positions in London,
Caulder Moore were asked to transfer
the concept to appeal to a potential
Middle East market in Dubai. Using
the unique Gina motif, a distinctive
colour palette, bespoke items and
luxury finishes, the resulting design
for the interior incorporated the premium
values of the footwear brand. The
ultra-glamorous, iconic and highly
opulent look – created using black
gloss, stainless steel, suede, velvet,
full-length mirrors and Swarovski
chandeliers – reflects the quality
of the luxury merchandise.

: CAULDER MOORE
On the right-hand side of the area
an arch in the shape of the iconic
GINA shoe motif set into a black,
glitter-clad wall, inlaid with
champagne suede and holding
black velvet display pads, leads
through to the couture area.

Branding and identity Selling the brand

Concept stores

The concept store is a place where new retailing ideas are tested or promoted for the first time in a specific location. The site is usually a key retail space with a high footfall and sales activity. The aim is to see if the new store concept achieves a good response from the public who would usually buy into the brand and if a new breed of consumer can also be attracted. The success or failure of a new concept is judged quite crudely in sales figures. If sales go up, then the concept is a success. There are cases, however, where the concept store in a major location is successful, but a roll-out into smaller sites may not work. This is because in poorer areas, the implementation of a polished new scheme may indicate a more expensive level of product that may appear unobtainable, therefore resulting in a downward turn in sales. For this reason, retailers are careful in understanding the market of a particular place in relationship to the brand, and can input the new concept at a more acceptable level.

Flagship stores

The job of the flagship store is to promote the brand in large, key retail sites around the world. The interior is often an extension of that found in a retailer's chain store, but produced to a higher specification and with unique features that act as a brand statement. The flagship store influences the brand choice made by the consumer through creating an exhibition-like experience that is more like a tourist attraction than a place to shop. The idea is that the consumer will visit a flagship store, may or may not purchase goods, but by visiting, they buy into the brand and may shop in the retailer's other stores closer to home. The flagship store is a clever marketing tool and aims to subconsciously stimulate the consumer into choosing a particular brand.

= **LEVI'S FLAGSHIP STORE**
Berlin, Germany

DESIGNER
= **CHECKLAND KINDLEYSIDES**

DATE
= **2008**

Checkland Kindleysides' brief was to create the ultimate retail brand experience for Levi's in Germany. An existing three-storey building with its striking arched windows provides glimpses of the brand within. Using each area to convey a distinct message, the designers worked to create a store that expresses the different personalities of the brand. On the ground floor, products are displayed alongside works from local artists; a beautiful curved staircase lends itself as a backdrop and displays a timeline, allowing customers to immerse themselves in the pioneering spirit of Levi's; and on the second floor, a series of rooms allows customers to explore a 'denim vault', displaying the rarest product, with staff acting as curators. The intention was to create a space where the relationship between Levi's and local artists, musicians and film-makers could be nurtured and exhibited, generating a youthful mix of global and local creativity.

Branding and identity   Selling the brand

Pop-up stores and events

One phenomenon currently gripping retail culture is the pop-up store or installation, which is a derivative of guerrilla marketing. The idea is that a store will appear in a location for a minimum amount of time. It may be in the form of a temporary structure or a space that is not usually associated with retail. The venue and event is not advertised, aiming the concept at the cool, those in the know. The pop-up store concept is associated with cutting edge and being with the 'in' crowd: 'if you don't know about it, you don't need to know' type of psychology. This concept is realised to lift the status of the brand and will provide the consumer with a different type of product that can only be found in this exclusive temporary location.

= **LEVI'S POP-UP STORE**
Various locations

DESIGNER
= **CHECKLAND KINDLEYSIDES**

DATE
= **2008**

This portable retailing concept for Levi's allows the brand to bring the product to the consumer, wherever they may be. The entire concept of merchandising, graphics, product and even changing room folds away to be stored within a series of flight cases, reminiscent of those that a band would take on tour; allowing the brand to be both agile and spontaneous, generating an element of exclusivity and surprise.

Lifestyle stores

The concept of the lifestyle store was derived from the idea that chain stores could provide a diverse product range under one brand. This was seen as being aspirational for the consumer, as they could then buy into a whole lifestyle experience. The lifestyle store can incorporate all of the retail sectors by offering fashion, homeware and entertainment departments. The lifestyle store sometimes sees the merger of diverse retailing, such as a bank with a coffee house, or a sports store with a technology area.

= **M&S LIFESTORE**
Gateshead, UK

DESIGNER
= **JOHN PAWSON**

DATE
= **2004**

The M&S Lifestore incorporates a diverse product range under one roof, making it a 'lifestyle' store. Characteristic of John Pawson, this particular design explores how architecture may be shaped around rituals of use rather than conventions of form. It draws on the essential Pawson vocabulary of wide floorboards, quiet white walls, floating benches, the shadow gap, floor-to-ceiling glazing with minimal frames, the optimal treatment of light and a restricted palette of natural materials.

Photographer: Richard Davies

Branding and identity   Selling the brand

Endorsements, collaborations and sponsorships

It is usual for brands to be seen sponsoring major events, such as sports competitions, in the form of advertisement hoardings. More recently, brands collaborate with artists of different types as a way of promoting the brand in particular circles, therefore enhancing its attraction. In recent years, we have seen a rise in celebrities endorsing products with their name, which in turn is their brand, to raise the status of a product type and to give the consumer the opportunity to, in some small way, become them. The sale of perfume is a good example of this.

Whether the brand is a celebrity endorsement, collaboration between the arts and brand or sponsorship of an event, the outcome impacts on the interior space for its duration. The space in some cases becomes a one-off event in itself or a temporary interior installation becomes the centre point of the store or gallery. This communicates an air of exclusivity to consumers who are quick enough and in the know, enabling them to buy into the brand for a limited period or to experience the brand as an installation rather than a place to shop.

= **SONY PLAYSTATION® EVENT**
Various locations

DESIGNER
= **CHECKLAND KINDLEYSIDES**

DATE
= **2007**

To celebrate PlayStation's six-month season of arts collaborations with the Baltic, English National Opera and British Film Institute, an iconic interactive installation was designed and moved to different venues. The mirrored sculptural form was developed to enhance its surroundings and reflect the rich visual content of each venue.

Branding and identity Student case study

PROJECT
= **MOBILE PHONE STORE**

DESIGNER
= **MAGDALENA KUMALA**

DATE
= **2006**

= Computer-generated
visualisations of the
completed space.

= Plans of
the space.

! Students were asked to design a retail
space for the display, selling and storage
of a luxury brand of mobile phone,
incorporating a strong brand identity that
can be easily recognised and accepted
throughout the world. This resulting design
considers the variety of product ranges
and the number of phones to be displayed.
The site used for the project is based on
a typical retail unit in a shopping mall of
approximately 40 square metres and a
ceiling height of three metres with adequate
storage for 70 phones. The sales process
allows staff to engage with customers
once they have shown interest in a specific
product, with space where the staff and
customer can sit down to discuss the
phones comfortably. The design concept
is based on opulence, seduction and
exclusivity and uses luxurious materials
and lighting to suggest the quality of
the product and to mimic the identity of
the brand.

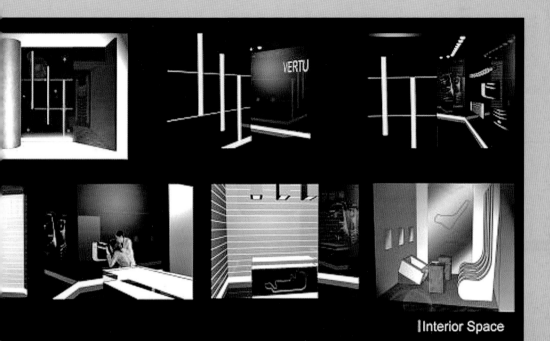

Interior Space

Now imagine that you have been asked to design a retail space for the display, storage and selling of a luxury brand of mobile phone.

List other mobile phone brands. What makes yours original?

Could these qualities be echoed in the design of the space? How?

List the requirements of a space of this nature. Can the qualities of the brand be reflected in these elements?

What elements can be carried across other branches?

The mobile phone industry is fast-paced and competitive. How could your design be easily updated?

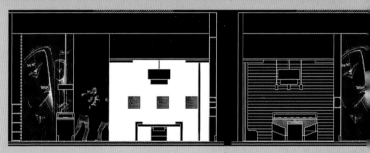

= Sections of the space.

Retail spaces can be defined and identified through different retail sectors. These sectors can be broadly described as food – the evolution of the market into supermarket and speciality food stores; fashion – clothing, shoes, accessories and beauty products; home – DIY, furniture, fabrics and cookware; and leisure and entertainment – sport, technology, travel and finance. Each sector has been influenced through social and economic conditions, politics, history and the development of design processes.

THIS CHAPTER aims to identify these influences on the designed space of each sector and explain the nature of the evolving retail experience. This is demonstrated by examining leading examples in retailing in each sector.

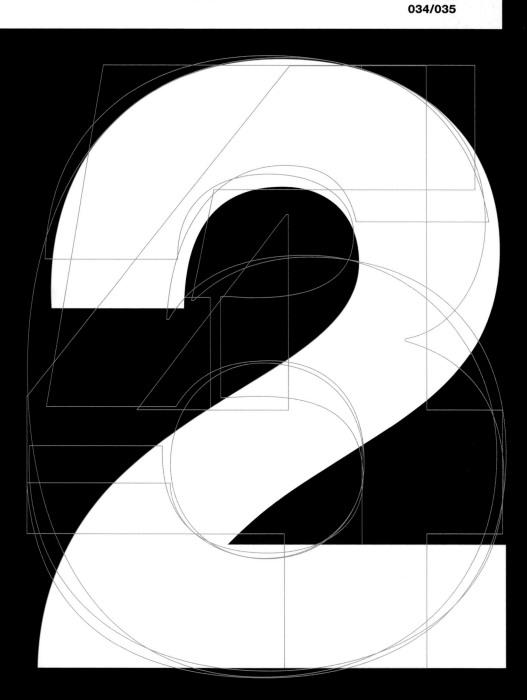

Retail sectors Food

Food retail is a huge industry, evident in every town and city through its cafés, restaurants, coffee shops and supermarkets. Today, large conglomerates and retail chains dominate food sales in the Western world, with many well-known brands pitching against each other and independent retailers for local trade.

The design language of these retail environments, often repeated from town to town, can at first appear monotonous, yet for many of us they are part of our everyday routine for sustenance. Delve deeper into the concepts of such spaces and an interesting process begins to emerge. These spaces have derived from cultural influences and worldwide traditions, and have been interpreted into a systematic, functional store environment. For instance, many coffee shops and restaurants reflect European café culture, taking advantage of the warm climate with open facades and exterior seating; similarly, supermarket product displays are reminiscent of street markets and old market halls, with produce stacked high, and the colours of food and packaging utilised to attract sales. The layout of aisles too, pushing customers in a particular direction, is set out in a similar way to the market, but in a much more regimented manner.

= **DJEMMA EL FNAA SQUARE**
Marrakesh, Morocco

Many cities are centred on the market. Here, the scent of herbal medicines and incense fills the air, creating a unique ambience associated with Morocco. The market merges into the many alleyways leading off it, where trading continues from the souks. In markets such as this, the produce sells itself.

= **FLOATING MARKET**
Bangkok, Thailand

The floating fruit and vegetable market in Bangkok is an example of bringing food into the city by whatever means necessary.

Markets

Historically, the marketplace has played a major role in the emergence of cities, from the covered markets of Central Asia and China, the Arab souk, the Roman forum to the street markets and marketplaces of European cities. Markets are traditionally the places where food and other essential items were brought into the city from the surrounding farmland or from the sea to be sold to the masses. The trade routes for the transportation of such produce have been instrumental in creating communities in the form of villages and towns along the way.

In many countries, the market is still the hub of the city. It is a place for engagement, creating a buzz with its richness in activity, sounds, colours, smells and experience. The market is transient, ever changing, and is part of the urban landscape.

Market stalls are constructed from simple frames to allow for flexibility, disassembly and storage. Each stall is like a little shop with the awning overhead creating an interior space and sheltering goods from the elements. They are functional and allow for the display of goods at table height, with containers of food piled high, and hanging for textiles. Here it is the produce that sells itself rather than the design of the display.

Market halls

In the West, market halls were built as a way of housing market traders and sheltering them from the elements on the streets. In the 1980s, many market halls in the UK changed use or were demolished, as supermarket shopping became the norm. When the City of London was originally built, the strategy had been to meet the essential needs of all of the residents of the city and as a result, London had a wealth of sizeable wholesale markets: Smithfield's for meat and Billingsgate for fish (both of which are still running today). Borough Market, Covent Garden Market and Spitalfields Market were used for selling fruit and vegetables (only Borough remains as a food market). The market hall has seen a re-emergence in recent years and although it has lost its core value, it is now a tourist destination and a place for finding specialist high-quality ingredients, arts and crafts, textiles and fashion.

The layout of the market hall tends to be based on rows of permanent shop accommodation overlooking a central open market space for pitching stands.

: R. THORNE
Markets were 'intended to serve bodily needs as the church served spiritual ones'.

? **HISTORY AND NARRATIVE**
Established practices and historical uses can dramatically inform the design of a retail interior. An aura of the past can affect user experience and can be regarded as a design tool of great worth. These issues are dealt with in greater detail in the AVA title, *Basics Interior Architecture: Context + Environment*.

= COVENT GARDEN MARKET
London, UK

Covent Garden's Jubilee Hall in London, UK, consists of two open market squares, with three rows of shops, fronted by colonnades on each side. Square lodge houses, originally intended to be used as pubs or coffee houses, stand at each end. The hall also has two terraces overlooking the market squares, which were to be used for exclusive retail spaces to attract a higher class of visitor. Covent Garden's Jubilee Market Hall was regenerated in the 1970s and is now famous for its Arts and Crafts market: a major tourist attraction. Spitalfields Market has also recently been regenerated (completed in 2005) and now contains a contemporary steel and glass insertion, housing cafés, restaurants and upmarket shops.

Supermarkets

The need for markets was eradicated in most of the Western world due to the rise of the supermarket in the mid-1920s. Large conglomerates now ship food of all types around the world to fulfil the needs of the masses. This food tends to be cheap, easily accessible, and readily available and does not depend on the seasons to grow. This convenience helps to sustain our modern lifestyles: long working hours and the move of women away from the home and into the workplace.

Supermarkets are now a destination for all types of retail coming together under one roof. The supermarket environment is felt by many to be somewhat clinical; it is logical and organised in a way that is easy to navigate. Signage and packaging are generic and bold. Aisles are wide and continuous. Produce is stacked high and plentiful, giving the impression of a warehouse. Fruit and vegetables are grouped together and displayed as in markets, using their colour as a selling point.

The supermarket experience is now a familiar environment that provides essential needs. The relationship between supermarkets and markets is evident in the reason for their existence and the translation of product display, but in many ways, they are opposites. Supermarkets do not recreate the sense of community in cities and social engagement that a market does and could not be described as the hub of a city. What the supermarket does do, however, is enable the maintenance of the current pace of living with its convenience, in an environment that is contemporary and fulfilling of aspirations.

Consumerism The purchase of material possessions.

Speciality food stores

The design of some speciality food stores can be more easily directly linked to the experience of the market than supermarkets can. Displays are more purposeful in creating an authentic market atmosphere and do not have the constraints of the large conglomerate chain. Like some market halls of today, these spaces bridge both the retail and leisure sectors; the products are an aspiration and create an impression of a lifestyle. They can combine a mix of contemporary and traditional interiors with character and charm.

= **VILLANDRY STORE**
London, UK

DESIGNER
= **DALZIEL AND POW**

DATE
= **2007**

Villandry bridges the retail and leisure markets through its gourmet food experience and French inspiration. The interior space is divided into a food hall, deli, charcuterie and a high-quality takeaway. The concept builds on the charm and heritage of the brand, creating a robust and feasible identity that can easily be traced back to the routes of the market space. The space is arranged so that the takeaway area is easily accessible from the street and the Food Hall is the central space with glimpses of the restaurant and bar beyond. The market feel is brought up to a sophisticated level through the interior detailing and graphic language used within.

Retail sectors Fashion

Fashion has an important influence on the retail sector. First, the interior space is designed in line with current trends in colour, material and graphics. Secondly, the sector is dominated by the huge consumer boom in the fashion industry, which covers the sales of clothing, accessories and shoes as well as beauty products. Fashion is a market that is largely dominated by women and is very much an interactive social experience perceived by many as a day out.

Fashion has played an important role throughout history in portraying class, wealth and heritage. However, fashion retail really took off with the birth of the department store concept in Britain. In Paris in 1850, this was developed into a shopping experience for the sophisticated Bourgeois, with the launch of the *Grand Magasin*, Le Bon Marché. The diverse product ranges and fashions represented the Bourgeois culture's commitment to appearance and material wealth, which is mirrored in the displays around the department store.

As the world of fashion is ever changing, fashion stores demand interiors that will appeal to the appropriate market. Fashion retail can be broken down into three areas: premium fashion labels, where innovative, cutting-edge fashions and retail spaces lead the way for their counterparts; boutiques, where the interior space is unique and styled to suit the needs of the individual; and the mass-consumed commercial fashion empire, where fashions and interiors are fast paced, exciting and sometimes controversial.

= **CALVIN KLEIN STORE**
Paris, France

DESIGNER
= **CLAUDIO SILVESTRIN**

DATE
= **1997**

The design of this space provides a simple, minimalist interior, common in many premium fashion stores. Using limestone floors, white walls and satin glass screens, the space is given a 'showcase' feel and is unable to detract from the clothes on display.

Retail sectors Fashion

= **COMME DES GARÇONS**
New York, USA; Tokyo, Japan and
Paris, France

DESIGNER
= **FUTURE SYSTEMS**

DATE
= **1998**

In 1998, Future Systems were asked to create stores
for Comme des Garçons in New York, Tokyo and
Paris. Their brief – to create a 'new kind of space with
an atmosphere of experimentation' – resulted in
three strong and unique designs. In New York, an
unusual mix of old and new was used to create a
natural and raw yet mechanical and machined finish.
In Tokyo, a curious filter between outside and inside
was created using two glass cone-shaped facades.
And in Paris, the historic façade is protected by a
sheer skin of pale pink glass. It is through these
unusual environments that the relationship between
space and clothing is established.

The fashion house

The fashion house is a term that is used to describe an exclusive fashion label, which has a designer or collection of designers working under its name. The premium fashion interior has become the most influential and creative of retail spaces and has fuelled a fertile fusion of fashion and architectural design. The large fashion houses often implement their major brand stores in London, Paris, Milan and New York, as these are considered the most prestigious fashion capitals of the world.

: REM KOOLHAAS

Shopping is a phenomenon that has 'remained mysteriously invisible to the architectural eye ... as one of the most critical and ... important contributions to urban texture at this moment'.

There are numerous displays of successful collaborations between fashion designers, artists, designers and architects, resulting in exciting and innovative retail spaces. This form of collaboration started in the 1980s, with minimalist stores created by leading architects coming to the forefront in retail design. These spaces were well crafted and detailed, often referred to as 'white boxes', in which clothing could be displayed like pieces of art. Today, we can still see examples of such interiors, but there is also a different type of space that has emerged. With the influence of cyberspace, the use of CAD modelling computer packages has transformed the design process in such a way that organic architectural forms are easier to manipulate and are being showcased as insertions into retail spaces.

The relationship between the fashion designer and architect allows the fashion designer to gain a strong, unique identity that the architect is able to realise in a quick timeframe. It is interesting to note that although these spaces exist, it is a trend that is not commonplace in architectural circles. In some cases, the architect will design a building for the fashion house, or work primarily on the interior of an existing building. The fashion house, in most cases, has a large budget and can therefore push the boundaries of contemporary design.

Retail sectors Fashion

The boutique

The rise of the boutique as a small independent retailer began in the late 1950s, in the aftermath of the Second World War, when the youth of that era was ready to embrace freedom and self expression. Before this time, a boutique was a department found in a larger store that provided clothing ranges somewhere between custom-made couture clothes and cheap mass-produced wholesale clothes. The first of these revolutionary independent shops to appear in the UK was called Bazaar and showcased clothes by the designer Mary Quant, on the Kings Road in London. It was designed and implemented by Terence Conran. The shop was innovative in the way that it manipulated space in a cool and contemporary way. It had a full-height glass facade that allowed the consumer to view the activities of the shop from outside. This was radically different from most retail spaces of that time and became symbolic of the rise of youth culture, which took place in the 1960s. Although Bazaar was influential in this mini revolution, its clientele mainly consisted of the wealthy and elite.

The boutique as we know it today houses custom-made or one-off speciality pieces – a far cry from the most prominent brand stores in the premium market place. The interiors are small, considered and individually designed to suit the image of the clothing and accessories.

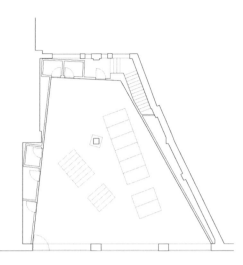

= **OKI-NI BOUTIQUE London, UK**

DESIGNER
= **6A ARCHITECTS**

DATE
= **2002**

Oki-Ni sell exclusive custom-made clothes from design houses such as Evisu, Levi's and Adidas. The interior scheme of its London store is based on an oak 'tray' that acts like a stage, with piles of felt layered to create platforms for product display. Oki-Ni has offered the fashion market a fresh relationship between consumer and product. Limited edition clothes by global and independent brands are available exclusively online from Oki-Ni. 6a architects won the commission to design the flagship store on Savile Row with an installation-based concept that emphasises the tactile and social opportunities of clothes shopping. Low piles of felt replace the traditional arrangement of shelving, rails and furniture, and define Oki-Ni's physical landscape; the generous felt surfaces are both display and furniture. This departure from the established conventions of retail design creates a place where resting and socialising play a critical part in the discovery of new products.

? **REPRESENTATION**

Representation of space is central to all aspects of interior design. Sketches, hand drawings, technical drawings and computer generated plans and models are all used by designers to communicate ideas to the client. The AVA title, *Basics Interior Architecture: Drawing Out the Interior*, looks at this in greater detail.

Retail sectors Fashion

Commercial fashion

Barbara Hulanicki invented the concept of mainstream fashion stores when she opened Biba in London, UK, in 1964.

Today, commercial fashion is dominated by chain stores with numerous identical shops in major towns and cities. The offer is available from every high street and is affordable to the masses. These shops often take reference from premium fashion brands in terms of both clothing collections and interiors. They are frequently changed to evolve with consumer expectations and because of the high level of activity, the interior finish becomes easily tired and dated. The interiors are varied, using materials, lighting and graphics to create an illusion. Retail designers work with marketing experts to focus the store's identity and relationship to the brand. In a heavily saturated market, being competitive in style and price is the key to success.

Chain stores
These are retail outlets sharing the same brand and management across locations.

= **TOPSHOP**
New York, USA

DESIGNER
= **DALZIEL AND POW**

DATE
= **2009**

Topshop is one of the UK's leading commercial fashion retailers. The launch of their New York flagship store in 2009 marked the transition to global brand. Replicating many of the design features found in UK stores, Dalziel and Pow have created a bold and confident statement and have successfully carried the brand across to the US market.

: BARBARA HULANICKI

I didn't want to make clothes for kept women ... I wanted to make clothes for people in the street ... I always tried to get prices down, down, down to the bare minimum.

Retail sectors Home

Consumer culture emerged in America in the 1950s following the Second World War. The focus of advertising was on enticing women back into the home after working in factories, filling jobs vacated by servicemen fighting abroad. The home featured predominantly in the role of the suburban housewife and kitchen gadgets and appliances became must-have items.

The Festival of Britain, held in 1951, was a celebration of Britain's past, present and future and saw the launch of the new 'Contemporary Style', which was derived from the American design, but was embedded with British traditions. The Council of Industrial Design (later to become the Design Council), led by Sir Gordon Russell, pioneered the role that designers were to play in society during these post-war years. The Contemporary Style was successful in its campaign aimed at British women. Furniture could be bought from a small number of high-street retailers. It was designed to suit the space within new government-owned houses and flats that were being built at that time. Interior decoration and home DIY were becoming Britain's post-war pre-occupation, and therefore the need for paint, wallpaper, flooring and furniture had a positive impact on the retailing industry.

Homeware and mass consumerism

Britain first came in contact with the
flat-pack concept in the early 1960s
when Terence Conran launched his own
furniture collection, Habitat. Conran's
aim was to introduce his commercial
furniture range to the domestic market
and was a reaction to the lack of good,
affordable furniture shops in the UK at
that time. Influenced by the markets
and shops of France and Northern Italy,
the store became very successful in
bringing a diverse range of inexpensive
lifestyle products to the high street.
Some of the cookware products had
never been seen on the British market
before. The pots, pans and other
cookware items were stacked high as
on the European market stalls, and this
has now become recognisable as the
Habitat retail concept.

In 1974, during the recession in the
West, Habitat launched its first Basics
range – a collection of 100 home
products at very low prices. The range
was a huge success and enabled the
company to attract a new clientele as
well as ride out the recession. When the
idea was re-launched in 1982, Habitat
was franchised in Japan. The Japanese
loved the Basics idea and asked for
permission to launch the concept under
a different name. The concept store
Muji was born and is now a leading
retailer of 'no-brand' products that are
simply packaged and sold cheaply
with the emphasis on recycling and
'no-waste'.

= **HABITAT IN THE 1960s**

The interior of one of
the first Habitat stores
in the UK.

: TERENCE CONRAN

**... a better style of life should be more
widely available. Habitat showed that
you need to follow the same philosophy
right through from drawing board,
via manufacturing, to the retail shop
floor .... This is what Habitat achieved
in the 1960s ....**

Retail sectors Home

IKEA and the birth of flat-pack

As interest increased in the design
of the home, the need for mass-
produced product ranges grew.
The biggest innovation in furniture
design of the late 1940s was flat-
pack furniture by the Swedish
designer, Gillis Lundgren. IKEA later
went on to develop their store concept
around this idea and opened the first
store in Sweden in 1958. The idea
was to promote cheap, mass-
produced furniture and homeware
that was easily accessible. The flat-
pack furniture is easy to store and
assemble, thus affecting the sale
price and the design of the showroom.
The IKEA store as we know it consists
of a showroom, marketplace and
warehouse. The idea of the layout is
that the customer walks a particular
long route so that they view all
of the products and room sets for
inspiration, and note down the
reference of the furniture they wish
to buy. There are, however, short
cuts through the space. Then, the
customer has to walk through the
marketplace, where products can
be picked up, into the warehouse,
where they select their furniture
before paying for their items. This
spatial structure was new to retailing
and promoted mass-consumerism
and accessibility.

Premium home stores

In contrast to the domestic furniture
retailers on the high street, another
breed of furniture and homeware
manufacturers targets the high-end
market. This market sees the
celebrated famous furniture and
product designer at the forefront
of the retail experience, with iconic
pieces being sold, much like pieces
of art, in both the domestic and
commercial sectors.

= **DROOG**
New York, USA

DESIGNER
= **STUDIO MAKKINK AND BEY**

DATE
= **2009**

The design for this store breaks
the norm of retail design. The brief
was to create an interior installation
made up of elements that can
be purchased. Jurgen Bey's
'House of Blue' takes this one
step further. Products are
displayed as if in a gallery; parts
of the interior are also for sale.
They can be bought as seen or
can be custom-made or fitted to
the customer's requirements.

? **ELEMENTS AND OBJECTS**
Objects can be used in the retail space to great
effect. These objects can be small or large, new
or found and can add great character to a space.
Designers are currently using such techniques to
further establish a brand within a retail space.
The use of objects in interior space is looked at in
greater detail in the AVA title, *Basics Interior
Architecture: Elements/Objects*.

Retail sectors Leisure and entertainment

= **REEBOK FLASH STORE**
New York, USA

DESIGNER
= **FORMAVISION**

DATE
= **2002**

Recently, Reebok re-invented itself in a new consumer offer. The Reebok Flash Store opened in New York for a limited period in the CV2 Contemporary Art Gallery, selling retro and limited edition footwear. Formavision, whose trademark is to use art as part of their interior scheme, designed the space.

The leisure and entertainment sector has grown significantly in the last ten years. Whether the activity is based around a destination or a product purchase, the chances are the interior space will encapsulate a brand. An outing to the cinema, museum or theatre will each give an opportunity to buy into the experience through a shop, bar or café.

The leisure sector includes sport – as an activity or apparel; technology – sound, audio and gaming; travel – modes of transport and travel agency; and finance – the services of banks and building societies. Banks are now abandoning the high street and going online.

Retail sectors Leisure and entertainment

= **APPLE STORE**
New York, USA

DESIGNER
= **BOHLIN CYWINSKI JACKSON**

DATE
= **2006**

The Apple Store, New York, occupies an
underground retail concourse with entry through
a 10-metre-tall glass cube at street level. Housing
a transparent glass elevator and staircase, the
cube entices customers down into the retail space
below. By day it acts as a natural skylight; by night
it lights up as a sign. Carefully tailored steel, stone
and wood fixtures and fittings all combine to create
the perfect backdrop to Apple's state-of-the-art
technology and an iconic piece of architecture on
the New York street.

Technology

The use of technology in the home and workplace has seen a phenomenal increase as advancements have taken place and products have become the must-have gadgets of the moment. Products such as mobile phones, games consoles, MP3 Players and home computers have taken the high street by storm, creating a new breed of shops geared towards the technologically minded and youth market. Many of these brands are global and need an interior space and graphic language that will appeal on all levels.

Apple Mac computers have long been the favoured tool of choice for design professionals. In 1998, the iMac was released and became the fastest-selling desktop computer in history. In 2001, the iPod was launched and became the leading MP3 player, setting a precedent for other manufacturers. In the same year, Apple opened its first retail store in San Francisco and Washington DC. The Apple Store now exists globally and reinforces the Apple brand. The stores are revolutionary in the technology sector and focus on being user-friendly and an environment where products can be tried and tested. The stores have a children's section, a 'genius' bar, a theatre and a solutions centre as part of the store concept.

The mobile phone is also now a mainstream essential product. Mobile phone stores are commonplace on the high street and often offer a personal service with consultation areas, exhibition-like displays and brand messages. The need for the consumer to keep up with technology means that mobile phones are regularly replaced, keeping the market strong and competitive.

: JAMES GARDNER
The new plaza in front of the General Motors building on Fifth Avenue at 59th Street is a triumph of urban design... Suddenly, as if out of nowhere, New York has a new public space that will prove to be a source of civic pride and aesthetic delight.

= **PORSCHE SHOWROOM**
Leusden, Netherlands

DESIGNER
= **QUA**

DATE
= **2004**

The new scheme for the Porsche showroom in Leusden was intended to reflect the passion and emotion of the brand. It needed to include a lounge area, bar, atelier, shop, reception, and delivery area, whilst retaining the maximum number of cars inside the showroom. The design shows the rich racing history of Porsche, the luxury of the cars, their technical and engineering qualities, and is inclusive of non-owners enthusiastic about the Porsche brand. By using long, low shapes, a colour palette of blacks, metals and whites, the design emphasises the curves of the cars and the material and technical sophistication of the Porsche brand.

Travel

The motor industry is undergoing major changes in the way it trades. The car showroom and forecourt as we know it is said to be disappearing. Today, car manufacturers are jumping on the branding bandwagon and are creating retail experiences for the consumer. Flagship stores are emerging with exhibition spaces, cafés and restaurants as part of the offer. Buying a car these days is about buying into a lifestyle, rather than buying a commodity that will get you from A to B. The future of car retailing is said to be in showcasing cars to specific market audiences rather than having physical showrooms. This idea leads to the purchase being made online. The effect of this radical shift will see the car showroom disappear from the high street. Car sales will become friendlier towards the public and less corporate in their selling techniques.

Other aspects of travel retail concern the holiday market. Although travel agencies can still be seen on the high street, many holiday purchases are made online. Customers are able to search numerous databases and custom-make their own holidays for a fraction of the price on the high street. Leading dot com companies such as <www.lastminute.com> have transformed this retail sector to the benefit of the consumer.

Finance

The finance sector has seen two main shifts on the high street. The first is the collaboration of high street banks with other offers. In the UK, for example, Santander and Costa Coffee now share retail space, offering the customer a lifestyle experience; secondly, the rise in Internet banking and online purchases. This has directly affected the banking system, making banks more accessible to the public and bringing about the closure of many high-street premises. The remaining banks and building societies have changed their appearance to become more appealing to the general public and less formal and traditional in their presentation. They now rely more heavily on self-service.

: CHATEL, F. AND HUNT, R.

Car retailing of the future must be total retail therapy, otherwise 'The Dream' cannot be sustained …. And what about the existing car showroom? Expect that to be as rare as a bank on the high street in Britain by 2004.

Retail sectors Student case study

PROJECT
= **MARKET PLACE**

DESIGNER
= **JEKATERINA ZLOTNIKOVA**
STEPHANIE HARRIS
ANGELIKI IOANNOU

DATE
= **2009**

! Students were asked to design a marketplace that would bring together the different cultures and histories of the surrounding area while being used as a vehicle to explore the idea of sustainable communities through locally sourced produce. In this way, the project looked at creating bridges between user groups so that social interaction could take place, and at regenerating an existing building for its original use, whilst exploring the transient nature of space.

Students made careful consideration of light and colour, using the market and its products as a point of inspiration. They also carefully considered their use of materials, using only those that related to the context of the area and those that were locally sourced.

They explored the different strands of the marketplace, through urban analysis, geometric and structural analysis of the building, light analysis and ergonomics. Students also inserted pattern, threshold, people movement and people mapping as streams of thinking. They discovered ways of thinking about the transient nature of human occupancy and the temporary nature of human existence and how this can inform the design process.

The research, analysis and concept development formed the basis of the design project, with the user at the core of the design strategy.

= The market stall is the place where customer interaction takes place. By Jekaterina Zlotnikova.

= The garden is in the centre of the building and open to the elements. It provides the opportunity to grow produce to sell in the market. By Angeliki Ioannou.

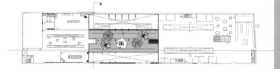

= This plan demonstrates circulation focused on pace – there is a slow meandering pace around the market stalls and a quick pace that takes visitors down the side of the building. By Stephanie Harris.

? Now imagine you have been asked to design a flexible market space.

1 How are these spaces used across the world? Where is your design located and how will this affect certain factors?

2 Are you trying to encourage or discourage certain behaviours? How will you do this?

3 Do you think this space will appeal to particular groups of people? How will you try to make the space more accessible and appealing to other groups?

The choice of space available to a retailer is vast in terms of location and type. Since the 1980s retail boom, developers have sought to take advantage of industrial wasteland and have regenerated disused spaces for retail purposes either away from the city centre or as a connection to an already established shopping area; or as a regeneration programme to bring character and life back into a barren urban setting. A retailer has an impact on the surrounding environment through their choice of site, and has a responsibility to adhere to local planning restraints, to consider the effect on local trade, and to evaluate noise, traffic and congestion issues that may arise from their positioning.

THIS CHAPTER **broadly examines the variety of sites available to retailers, from high street to shopping centre, and discusses a range of one-off scenarios. Each site maintains a different design approach that is influenced by both the context and the nature of the site.**

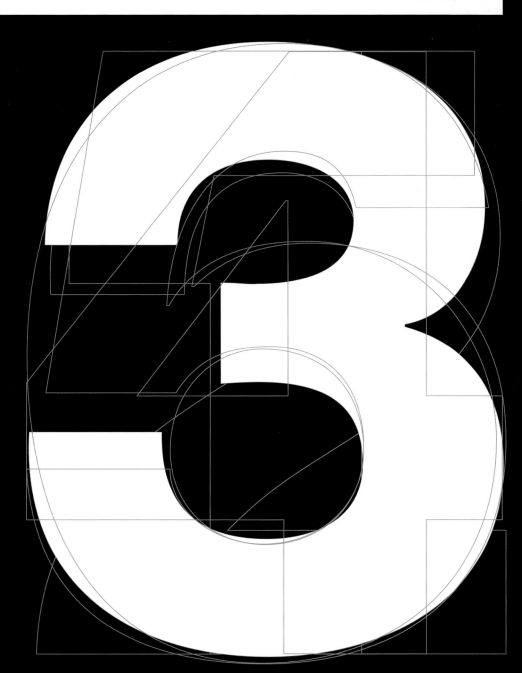

Retail sites Department stores

The popularity of shopping as a leisure activity took off in the nineteenth century with the rise of a British phenomenon: the department store. For the first time, huge arrays of products were available under one roof.

Before the department store, shops were highly specialised and expensive, with a low turnover and high overheads for non-food purchases. Drapery retailers began to see that the rationale of indoor food markets could work for the textile industry, in supplying products to a mass market. The layout was forever changing and growing as new lines were added, making the stores into the rambling spaces we still experience today. Later, buildings were purpose built and designed in a range of impressive architectural styles.

Today, the concept of the department store is still successful. It houses lifestyle merchandise from fashion and accessories, to haberdashery, home and cookware, to speciality food. The interior of the department store is controlled by an in-house team of designers whose job it is to dress window displays, design the layout of the store and its concessions, implement signage and other graphics, and maintain a cohesive scheme throughout the store.

= **HARVEY NICHOLS STORE**
Istanbul, Turkey

DESIGNER
= **FOUR IV**

DATE
= **2006**

This three-floor, 86,000-square-foot store, complete with food market and a 100-cover restaurant, showcases the very best in Western contemporary retailing, complemented by rich swatches of local material and the traditional skills of Turkish craftsmen. The design details are an exercise in exuberance. The fascia entrance is in polished black stone and gold embossing, the ground floor is virtually crystalline, and the lingerie area features a central chandelier of glass polished butterflies and high-pile carpet. Gilt, a 100-cover restaurant, sits atop the Harvey Nichols store. Serving international food in an environment featuring fine traditional handiwork, the restaurant itself is set to become a destination in its own right for Istanbul.

Retail sites Department stores

= **SELFRIDGES STORE**
Birmingham, UK

DESIGNER
= **FUTURE SYSTEMS**

DATE
= **2003**

Selfridges in Birmingham is famously known for its organic exterior, influenced by a dress designed by Paco Rabanne. The interior is centred on a roof-lit atrium space with escalators snaking up through the building. This department store is a good example of a contemporary building for retail.

Entrance, circulation and interior layout

The department store is first experienced from the pavement. The impressive facades dominate the high street with their grand exteriors and full-height glazing. Window displays are evocative and regularly updated, showing this season's latest fashion and must-have items.

The department store often has several entrances, making it more easily accessible. The journey into the department store, in most cases, begins with a central entrance foyer and atrium with stairs or elevators rising to each floor. The atrium is often impressive and spacious and acts as a meeting place or a starting point to the navigation around the store. The traditional staircases were curved and ornate, taking their influence from Parisian stores. Today, escalators are often seen in their place, with lifts also accessing each floor. Walkways are wide and clearly signposted. Each floor has strategically placed payment areas and fitting rooms, which work around concessions. The shopping experience is concluded with space to eat, meet and refresh.

New contemporary department store buildings are still based on traditional layouts, focusing on the central circulation space and relying on the concession scheme. The buildings are still monumental landmarks and places for social interaction.

Concessions

The selling space in a department store is split into concessions. This basically means that each space is let out to a different retailer. This creates the opportunity for fashion labels to sell alongside each other in one establishment, making the department store a one-stop place to shop. The retailer's design team implements concessions and the space is designed in line with the retailer's brand and other stores so that an identity is clear and constant.

Each concession requires its own cash counter, display elements such as gondolas, tables and wall fixtures, and must consider the adjoining junction to neighbouring retailers and walkways. Graphics and signage are an important component to setting each concession apart, and advertising the strength of the brand; these also aid customer navigation. Retailers are often grouped together depending on product type and relationship to each other; therefore the reputation of the brand or brands may attract the desired client base to the department store.

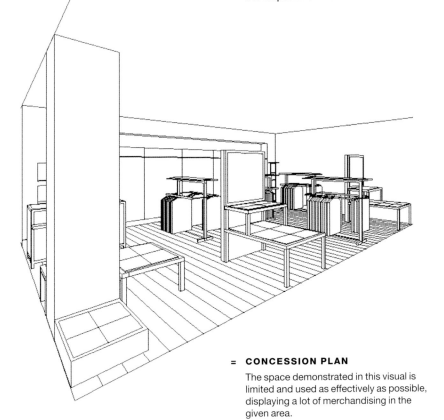

= CONCESSION PLAN
The space demonstrated in this visual is limited and used as effectively as possible, displaying a lot of merchandising in the given area.

Retail sites High street

The high street is the busiest central area for commerce in any town or city. These streets are connected by alleyways, arcades and department stores and are often defined by their architectural style.

Depending on the era in which a town or city was initially planned and constructed, the high street can take different forms. Older cities may have grandeur and a mixture of architectural styles, and buildings might be listed, carrying many restraints on structural changes. Older cities tend to be more meandering, having evolved over time. Newer cities and towns are much more structured in their urban plan, with the retail areas clearly defined and catered for in adequate buildings that do not carry many constraints. High-street retailers tend to fall loosely into one of these categories: boutiques or local traders, department stores or chain stores. The boutiques and local traders, in most cases, take the smaller retail units and can be found in the connecting alleys or arcades. The department store is housed in the largest buildings, and the chain stores take up everything in between.

: **RASSHIED DIN**
The approach was simple, the product was inexpensive and obtainable, and the formula was widely reproduced. The result was outlets that were instantly recognisable and far more accessible to most people than exclusive department stores.

Chain stores

In the Western world, high streets as we know them today are often criticised for having the same characteristics from location to location. Many believe this is because chain stores are rapidly wiping out the existence of independent retailers. The retail landscape is often repeated from city to city, engulfing the unique cultural and social qualities of each place.

The chain store was formulated as an alternative retail type to the department store and offered mass-produced goods at low prices, thus appealing to the working classes. Woolworths was one of the first recorded chain stores with its first store opening in New York in 1879. After 120 years of trading, Woolworths finally closed its doors in 2009, unable to compete with online retailing. Due to globalisation and the ease of importing/exporting and efficient travel, chain stores today are implemented worldwide.

The design of chain stores is in line with current design trends and takes inspiration from premium fashion stores, as discussed in Chapter 2. It does, however, tend to use a less expensive palette of materials and finishes. The interior schemes tend to last around six years before being completely replaced, but are often updated through the use of colour and graphics in between. Chain stores tend to work on three different cost levels in terms of the interior fit-out: high-spend, medium-spend and low-spend, depending on where the store is being implemented. Retail designers consider these three options when putting together a package of drawings for the interior space, and offer alternative arrangements and specifications to suit all three budgets. In all cases, there would be a selection of fixtures and finishes that would remain for all schemes, which are often main features such as the cash desk/servery area, for instance.

Roll-out

A term used to describe the reproduction of an interior scheme into a number of different sites. Although the scheme may need to alter to reflect the nature of the site, the principles behind the design idea remain the same.

= **HMV**
Concept store

DESIGNER
= **DALZIEL AND POW**

DATE
= **2009**

This chain store for HMV looks to implement its 'Next Generation Store' concept into a number of different sites from high street, to shopping centre, to concourse. The concept represents HMV's blueprint for the future of its retail offer, where the physical comes together with digital to create a compelling experience. At the front of the store is a one-stop shop, which houses the latest releases, charts promotional items and continuing the more accessible theme, there is a social 'hub' with IMacs for customers to browse the internet.

Retail sites High street

Arcades

The arcade as a public place for shopping, socialising, entertainment and political engagement, first emerged in Paris following the French Revolution, it was called the Palais Royal. An arcade can generally be defined as a passageway between shopping streets that is covered, usually by a glass and steel roof. The arcade comes in many different layouts and contains rows of shops on either side with storage space above. The idea of the arcade can be traced back to the passageways of the Eastern bazaars and traditionally provides space to smaller retailers and designer/makers. The architectural style of the arcade is incredibly ornate, with many fine examples still existing throughout the Western world. One of the most prominent features of the arcade is the glass atrium, which brings in natural light and connects the interior with the exterior. Each shop facade has the same architectural detail and retailers must keep to the design style in terms of graphics and signage.

: J.F. GIEST
If the nearby cathedral represents the body of Christ, then the arcade represents a kind of pantheon of bourgeois society... it is filled with the noise that incessantly flows through it.

= **GALLERIA VITTORIO EMANUELE II**
Milan, Italy

DESIGNER
= **GIUSEPPE MENGONI**

DATE
= **COMPLETED IN 1877**

This arcade is one of the finest examples of a public, covered promenade. The building was constructed between the cathedral and the Scala in the shape of a cross, in the centre of Milan. The photograph shows the attention to detail and the consistency in the designed frontages throughout, as well as the atrium shedding natural light into the space.

Retail sites Shopping centres

Shopping centres or malls were pioneered in America during the 1950s. The malls were built on the outskirts of the cities and had plenty of parking space and service areas for suitable access. The shopping centre has been criticised over the years for turning cities into 'ghost towns'; this is certainly evident in America.

In Britain, many shopping centres are built in the centre of the city and are the pinnacle of the shopping area, with the high street leading from them. The architecture of the early shopping centres was often made up of concrete structures that were oppressive and unfriendly, and many have now been replaced by airy glass and steel structures with impressive atriums and natural light flooding through to the interior. The design and build of a shopping centre is a good example of how architects, landscape designers and interior designers work together. The architect is responsible for the building scheme and working out the general circulation and division of space; the landscape designer specialises in planting in the malls and outdoor spaces, whilst the interior designer, often specialising in retail design, brings the building to life with theatre, lighting, finishes, seating and graphics. The role of the interior designer also extends to the fit-out of the retail units.

Circulation and layout

The experience of shopping in a mall begins in the car park, which is very accessible and sometimes in the basement of the building or to the rear. Upon entering the building, signage and graphics play a major role in aiding navigation. Maps and hanging banners are clearly visible and define the brand of the centre. Some malls are configured in straight rows and others are more meandering or have a circular navigation. Many are set out over a few floors with escalators and lifts connecting the spaces. The walkways are very wide and have planting and seating to break up the space. The shopfronts face on to the walkways and sometimes pop out to make them more visible.

The shopping centre generally comprises a number of different-sized shop units with 'anchor' stores at either end. The 'anchor' stores are typically well-known department stores that take up a large area of the shopping centre and act as a magnet to draw customers through the mall. Sometimes the anchor is a cinema or bowling alley. This all adds to the experience of a day out. A main food court is often a central feature with a good selection of traders and plenty of seating. Toilets, banking facilities and cafés appear at regular intervals. Shopping centres are accessible for families and sometimes have crèche facilities, as well as baby changing in the toilets and high chairs in the food halls and cafés.

? **RHYTHM**
The structural system of a building can help create an order or rhythm. A procession of repeated elements can help to set up this rhythm or an unusual object might be used to contrast with it. Rhythm is discussed in greater detail in the AVA title, Basics Interior Architecture: Form + Structure.

Retail sites Shopping centres

= **ZLOTE TARASY**
Warsaw, Poland

DESIGNER
= **THE JERDE**
PARTNERSHIP INC.

DATE
= **2007**

Shopping centres can bring new
life to urban areas. Zlote Tarasy,
a multi-level, mixed-use project
located in central Warsaw, serves
as a connection to the city, and
creates a model for further urban
redevelopment in the area. The
design takes its inspiration from
Warsaw's historic urban parks,
with an undulating glass roof,
organised terraces and generous
open spaces.

Retail units

Retail units in a shopping centre are fairly straightforward to fit out without having to adjust the architectural elements of the space. Unless the centre is new, an old scheme may have to be ripped out first, but this is usually non-structural. They are purpose built and always provide a rear door for deliveries and services, adequate space for storage adjacent to the delivery door, a discreetly positioned soil vent pipe connection for staff facilities, accessible electric hook-up and a position on the roof of the building or outside wall for air conditioning. The design of the unit has to be approved by the shopping centre management team and must adhere to the design guidelines of the centre, as well as usual building regulations. The shopfront design is the most contentious part of the design package, as it must work alongside the other traders without obscuring the view of its neighbours, and must sometimes include generic architectural details that are apparent throughout the malls. There is often very little natural light into the retail units, the only source being from the covered mall. Therefore, artificial lighting plays an important role in the whole retail scheme.

Retail sites Out-of-town shopping

= **A TYPICAL RETAIL OUTLET**
A typical retail outlet, partially
covered and with shopfronts and
signage protruding out on to
the walkway.

**Out-of-town shopping extends
far beyond the realms of the
shopping centre. The landscape of
many countries is scattered with
large warehouse-type buildings
that contain endless amounts of
merchandise. The advantage of
out-of-town shopping is in enabling
accessibility. Towns and cities are
often limited in parking space and
have heavy traffic congestion.**

The out-of-town experience has an
abundance of parking and is often
situated near major roads. The
downside, however, is the effect these
buildings have on the countryside and
the ever-decreasing areas of natural
beauty. There are traders that naturally
fit into out-of-town retail spaces, which
can be broken down into the categories
of retail outlet or villages, retail parks,
megacentres and hypermarkets.

: **N.K. SCOTT**
**The phenomenon of the out-of-town
shopping centre, the out-of-town
business park, leisure centre,
university or any other human
activity is singular to our age. The
reason is simple and a consequence
of the invention of the internal
combustion engine.**

Retail outlets

The retail outlet or village is designed around the idea of a shopping mall, and can be open to the elements or under a covered mall. The village will include a food court and the usual public conveniences alongside large retail units. The units are warehouse-like and often constructed from brick and steel with full-height glazed shopfronts. Retailers use these spaces for selling off excess stock at discounted prices. The interior fit-out of such units is often done on a low budget with little attempt to hide the industrial nature of the space. Elements of the retailer's branded interior will appear in terms of graphics, fixtures and finishes.

Retail parks and showrooms

For some retailers, the out-of-town location is the ideal solution for their product type. Large items such as furniture and DIY paraphernalia, cars, white goods, outdoor and gardening equipment all benefit from having easy access in terms of deliveries and storage. The warehouse-like spaces work well for displaying large items and creating lifestyle spaces such as room sets, that help the customer buy into the product. The units also work well as showrooms for cars due to the open plan nature of the space and large frontages for manoeuvring stock.

Retail sites Out-of-town shopping

= **PON CATERPILLAR SHOWROOM**
Leude, Netherlands

DESIGNER
= **QUA**

DATE
= **2003**

This project saw the rebranding of CAT, establishing the values, and applying them to the architecture and interior of a complete new building. The building includes a CAT shop as well as the only showroom for Caterpillar bulldozers in the world.

? **SUSTAINABILITY**
In the fast-paced world of retail, designers must pay particular attention to their use of materials and resources. Reusing and recycling as well as alternative methods of heating and cooling spaces are just some of the ways in which interior designers can help to reduce the damage they are doing to the environment. Sustainability and environmental issues are discussed in greater detail in the AVA title, *Basics Interior Architecture: Context + Environment.*

Hypermarkets

The hypermarket is a concept created by the major supermarket chains. Supermarkets are often positioned on the edge of a town or city with smaller 'express' versions in the city centre or at other points of high footfall. The hypermarket is a much larger version of the supermarket and carries a generous variety of products under one roof. The buildings are industrial-looking warehouses and contain everything from groceries to clothing, to white goods, homeware and gardening. The supermarket chains buy stock in bulk, which makes it cheaper, and they then pass some of this discount on to the customers. These spaces tend to be rambling and organised in the same way as the supermarket, with aisles of products stacked high and divided into categories depending on the product. Some hypermarkets are spread over two or more floors. Wide, long, angled travelators are used to take the customer between floors with shopping trolleys.

Megacentres

'Megacentre' is the term used to describe an out-of-town retail shopping centre of huge proportions. The megacentre offers thousands of parking spaces, several anchor stores and leisure facilities such as sports complexes, multi-cinemas and in some countries, water parks. The centres are open throughout the day and into the night, seven days a week. The megacentre is a derivative of the shopping centre and all the same rules about its design and circulation patterns apply.

Retail sites The concourse

Retail exists wherever there are consumers with time on their hands and money to buy. As the travel industry has developed, so has the opportunity to sell.

The concourse provides the retailer with an opportunity to supply a concessionary sample of stock to the masses that are simply passing through, *en route* to somewhere else, sometimes 24 hours a day. Train stations and airports particularly have volumes of space between platforms and gates that are ideal for the positioning of retail units. The concourse also aids the global success of a brand as retailers gain access to consumers from all over the world.

Retail units within a concourse are simple structures. Some are freestanding in the middle of the concourse, with glass around all sides acting as the shop window, whilst others are divided along lengths of walls by stud partitions. Units are usually roller shuttered for security when closed. The stock for each unit is often locked away elsewhere in a separate storeroom for maximum security, with some retailers removing their merchandise at night.

Train stations

Train station retailing suits particular product types relating to travel or gifts. In smaller cities, local trade can do well as the train station is often the beginning of a relationship between the consumer and the local area; the beginning or end of a journey. It would be familiar to see a leading chemist, a leading stationer, a leading fast-food brand and coffee shop available at most stations, however small, therefore providing essentials to the commuter or holiday-maker. In larger, more modern stations the concourse has been transformed into a full shopping experience. Sometimes, the station may lead into a shopping centre as part of the exit from the station.

Petrol and service stations

Service stations were introduced along major motorways to provide a break for the fatigued driver. They have a captive market and often raise their prices, as they do not have any direct competition. The choice and quality of products and services available in the service station is varied. Most service stations provide a shop for snacks and essentials, but the main income is from the sale of food and beverages. Like the train station and airport, fast-food brands are readily available alongside canteen-style dining.

Petrol stations have in more recent years developed partnerships with other retailers such as fast-food or coffee chains, combining the sale of petrol with forecourt retail potential. This was started as a reaction to large supermarket chains selling cheaper petrol and was a bid to win customers back to the forecourt.

Airports

Airports today have retail areas that could be described as shopping malls. Rows of units fill large areas of space with many leading brands available. The added bonus of airport shopping used to be that goods were duty free, but since this was abolished, airports have had to change their strategy in giving the traveller a shopping experience that is both satisfying and memorable. Airports were traditionally places for buying perfume, cigarettes and alcohol at discount prices. Today, airports are the ultimate example of destination shopping. Whole terminals are branded as a lifestyle shopping experience. To define the consumer market within an airport, you need to understand the type of traveller passing through.

A terminal that deals with long-haul flights for instance will have to appeal to the culture and social aspirations of different user groups and can cleverly adjust the products and pitch to suit.

Retail sites The concourse

= **BIZA FLAGSHIP
DUTY FREE STORE**
Manchester airport, UK

DESIGNER
= **HMKM**

DATE
= **2008**

HMKM were tasked with designing
a customer-focused identity and
environment for Biza, a retail offering
that would 'radically re-define the
UK airport shopping experience'.
Initially launched at Manchester airport,
the scheme is to be rolled out across
Newcastle and East Midlands airports
too. With a clear awareness of customer
needs and airport environments,
HMKM successfully created a unique
and exciting new experience. Their
holistic approach included attention to
customer flow, use of materials and
colour palette and a complementary
staff dress code. This was an important
total rebranding of the previous 'Alpha
Airport Shopping' and transformed the
way people shop within the duty-free
environment, creating a department
store feel.

: R. DIN
**Airports have... the advantage of
knowing who its customers are and
when they will be passing through
its doors; it is also in the almost
unique position of knowing its
customers' sex, age and nationality
from air-ticket sales, passport
information and flight destinations.**

Retail sites Alternative venues

The retail venue, rather than standing alone, can be intertwined with an event or exhibition and is often a destination point to signify the end of a journey around a gallery.

As well as the physical sites discussed in this chapter, retailing also happens from home. The home catalogue has been around for many years, but with the growth in Internet usage over the last decade, the majority of major retailers also have an online offer. Alternative venues outline these retail ventures and the gap they fill in the retail market.

Galleries and exhibitions

On any day out to a theme or leisure park, to see an exhibition or visit an art gallery, there will inevitably be a shop at the end of the journey that will allow you to buy into the experience or take home a souvenir. These shops are dedicated to selling very specific products and enhance the brand of the event. They are individually designed to suit the product type and market audience; in the case of exhibitions the shop content may be temporary and frequently changed to match the exhibition, needing flexibility in its fixtures and display.

Large, well-known museums and art galleries are beginning to take their brand out of the building and on to the high street, selling their merchandise to a wider audience as a concession in centralised department stores in major cities. Art galleries are competing with major bookshops to be the best destination shop for art books. This trend sees the leisure and entertainment industry take a leap towards retailing that has never been seen before.

Virtual shopping

The Internet has been the catalyst for the phenomenon that is virtual shopping. Consumers have access to virtual shops 24 hours a day and can buy almost anything globally, from the safety and comfort of their home. Not only is shopping available from a computer, but also from a television or mobile phone. No physical space is required, goods can be stored off site or can be made to order.

All major retailers have online shopping sites that allow the consumer to place orders and expect deliveries within days. Cheap overheads also mean a mass of independent retailers trade online. The website design is crucial to virtual shopping. It should be user friendly and must illuminate the brand clearly. Search engines play an important role in how many 'hits' the website has and all major retailers want their site to be at the top of the search list. The delivery service also plays a big role in the success of bringing customers back, as convenience is the key to Internet shopping.

The emergence of virtual shopping raises the question as to whether retailers need physical shops at all. The answer lies in understanding the human psyche and the difference between shopping for necessity and shopping for fun. Convenience shopping is a chore; fun shopping engages in social interaction and the event of a day out. Also, physical shopping engages our senses in a way that virtual shopping cannot, through trying on clothes, feeling the quality of fabric, or smelling the printed pages of a book.

? **SITE**
The site on which a retail space is situated can have an important effect on the space itself and the way in which the space is used. These effects are discussed in more detail in the AVA title, *Basics Interior Architecture: Context + Environment.*

Retail sites Student case study

PROJECT
= **FENDER CHAIN STORE CONCEPT**

DESIGNER
= **FAHIROOL ADZHAR MUHAMAD**

DATE
= **2009**

! This project takes on the regeneration of an existing Regency-style building and converts it into a concept store for instrument manufacturer Fender. In order to understand an existing building and to read its interior structure, research into the building's style and histories must take place. Secondly, the geometries and structure of the building and the ways in which the building is affected by its context must be analysed. Once this information is collected and condensed, the interior can be designed effectively.

The resulting interior focuses on material qualities to enhance the acoustics of the space, and the vertical circulation focuses on a central stair that weaves organically through the building.

? Imagine that you have been given an existing building in which to implement a retail interior.

1 What do you need to understand about the building in order to design a successful intervention?

2 What types of analysis would you need to undertake at the beginning of the design process?

3 How could you enhance an existing building through the interior scheme?

4 What specialists would you work with to collect the building's data?

5 What areas of the building might be affected by planning and building regulations?

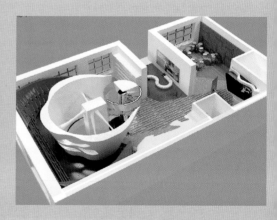

= The vertical circulation focuses on the central staircase.

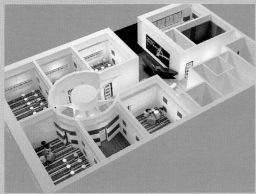

= Material qualities enhance the acoustics of the space. Seating takes its concept from the form of sound waves.

= Guitars and other instruments are displayed to their best effect on the ground floor so that customers can come straight into the retail space from the street.

The retail environment consists of the factors that play on the customer's senses in terms of sight, sound, smell and touch. This transpires through materials and their textures, the use of artificial lighting, the interior climate and the acoustic qualities of the space. The designer has a responsibility to be sensitive to the effects that design and building have on the environment and to minimise, where possible, waste and energy use. This, however, is not always under the designer's control, but considering these issues at the forefront of the design process can minimise risk to the environment further down the line.

THIS CHAPTER raises questions surrounding the ecological effects that retail and construction have on the environment and the ways in which they might be addressed.

The retail environment Retail and sustainability

The world of retail and its connection with consumption is often a controversial subject. Retail is about selling in large quantities, and in order to do this, manufacturing and mass-production is at the heart of the business. This uses vast amounts of materials and the Earth's resources in terms of energy, and creates carbon emissions that are harmful to the environment. Many manufacturers are beginning to address these issues, using materials that are organically grown and processes that are less harmful, but there is still a long way to go before these issues are resolved.

The built environment as a whole is associated with waste. Retail interiors are ripped out and replaced with every new tenant, or changed every five to seven years for a new concept. Also, during the building process, materials are wasted if not used and often end up in landfill rather than being recycled. As designers, part of our role is to consider the materials that are specified in terms of their ability to be reused or to last, or if recycled materials can be used instead. The designer and team of contractors can work together to eliminate waste and consider an alternative use for materials that are left over or changed.

In terms of energy consumption, electrical and mechanical engineers look carefully at the efficiency of their installations as part of the design process and produce documents that outline to the client the correct way to use the equipment. It is often the misuse of buildings and such equipment that can lead to energy waste.

BREEAM (Building Research Establishment Environmental Assessment Method) is a voluntary measurement rating for green buildings. Now widespread across Europe and the rest of the world, it was initially established in the UK. Its equivalents in other regions include LEED in the USA and Green Star in Australia. In terms of retail, their remit is to carry out assessments on new buildings; major refurbishments, tenant fit-outs; and management and operations assessment on existing buildings. They can look at the general display and sale of goods, food retail and customer service retail. The assessment aims to identify a score that measures the building or fit-out against a set of criteria that will identify any major concerns. Designers now work within the BREEAM guidelines, which in turn help them consider environmental issues.

An analysis of retail and its responsibility to the environment can be broken down into three areas of consideration: the building shell, the interior components and the building's energy consumption.

Interior shell

When considering the interior shell of a building, the key to being sustainable is to think through the interior structure and the choice of materials used. The first consideration should be whether the structure needs to be altered at all; is it useable in its current state? If not, care should be taken so that only minor alterations need to be made. Any structural work, building of walls (including those that are not supporting), the floor finish and ceiling finish is considered part of the interior architecture. Older properties in particular may have seen many structural adjustments in their lifetime so it is important to get the interior shell right structurally so that it should not have to be changed for a very long time. The key to this is to make the interior structure simple so that fixtures and fittings can be adapted around it. By considering the lifespan of the interior shell, the implemented design can have longevity, reducing the amount of building work over time, hence protecting the environment.

The materials used on the floor can also be adopted in this way. A terrazzo floor, for instance, could last 20 years if laid properly, as it is both neutral in appearance and durable. Using timber for the flooring also means that reclaimed materials can be reused. This may mean a marked or dented floor but it will again be durable and neutral.

: JUHANI PALLASMAA
We behold, touch, listen and measure the world with our entire bodily existence…. We are in constant dialogue and interaction with the environment, to the degree that it is impossible to detach the image of the Self from its spatial and situational existence.

The ceiling plane is an important element of the interior scheme as it houses many of the necessary electrical and mechanical components that make the space function (such as lighting and air conditioning). The architecture of the ceiling plane again can be considered as a fixed element that must be flexible enough in its design to meet the changing interior concept. The trickiest part will be the positioning of light fittings, as they may have to be moved to suit a new scheme.

In terms of sustainability, the more the existing interior can be kept intact the better. Minimising building work is essential.

? **REUSE**
In terms of sustainability, the reuse of old buildings is preferable to the creation of new ones. But it can also serve as a useful link to our cultural heritage and collective memory. Building reuse and its effect on the environment is discussed in greater detail in the AVA title, *Basics Interior Architecture: Context + Environment*.

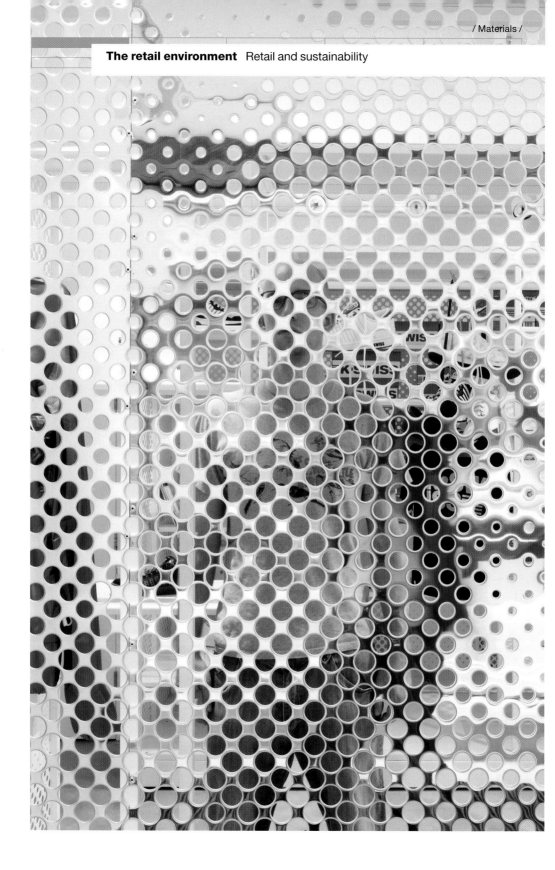

The retail environment Retail and sustainability

: 6A ARCHITECTS
Perforated polished stainless steel cladding elicts an ambiguous quality at the meeting point of reflection, transparency and opacity. The object reveals its contents through the perforations and mirrors the surroundings in its surface, creating a constantly changing installation.

= **K-SPACE CONCEPT STORE**
London, UK

DESIGNER
= **6A ARCHITECTS**

DATE
= **2008**

K-Swiss is a global sportswear brand renowned for its footwear; it also actively supports and promotes cultural events, especially live music and exhibitions. The brief was to produce K-Space – a retail space that located new and classic K-Swiss products alongside other culturally related objects (such as CDs and books) representing similar brand values. The key function of the space was its ability to transform at a moment's notice from a working retail space into an open, unbranded space for music or art events. The installation for both permanent and temporary spaces adapts a library archive storage system. Five of these units are specifically designed to combine display and storage and use slide-on tracks to reveal or conceal products.

Photographer: David Grandorge

Interior components

The components that furnish the interior – the fixtures and fittings that will drive the interior concept and layout – are often replaced on a five- to seven-year basis. This is because they simply wear out and may not meet the concept guidelines for a new interior scheme. Some can be refurbished and reused or adapted to suit a new scheme; others are thrown away and replaced. The key to reducing their environmental impact is through the materials. They could be constructed from recycled material or objects, for instance, or reclad to suit a new design scheme.

Energy consumption

The amount of energy it takes to run a retail unit or building is vast. The building is often climate controlled. The lighting consists of sometimes hundreds of fittings that are on for up to 12 hours a day, some 24 hours a day. Tills, music systems and cooking facilities all use large quantities of electricity and, in food retail, gas supply.

Cradle-to-cradle

This is a term used to describe the constant cyclical use of materials; the material is 'born', used, ripped out and reused.

The retail environment Materials

Hundreds of materials are available for use in the retail environment. Some are innovative whilst others are commonly found in every space. In terms of sustainability, certain materials can be used to lower the build's carbon footprint, although it is important to point out that this is still very much a grey area.

Interior designers work predominantly with materials, guaging how they look, feel and enhance the interior environment. The materials or sample board is first produced as part of the concept design and is discussed with the client. For every design project the material specification is formulated as part of the design scheme. The specification provides a detailed document of every material, the supplier and cost, as well as its ecological status.

Some materials have structural qualities that are used in the construction stage of the interior. Some materials lend themselves to creating the interior look through the fixtures and finishes. A diverse range of flooring solutions is available. They need to be durable as the amount of traffic moving through the interior space is high. It is also advantageous to think about the cleaning process and how materials will stand up to polishing machines and suchlike over time. In this chapter, the most common materials found in a retail environment are explored.

Timber

Timber is a versatile material that comes in a range of shades depending on the timber selected. It can be used as an interior wall cladding, for fixture and furniture construction or as a floor finish. It has warmth and is full of imperfections, which can add character to a space. Softwoods, mainly pine, are most commonly used for timber-framed fixture carcasses, with an outer skin applied for finishing. Hard woods such as oak, ash, beech, walnut, cherry and maple are more commonly used for flooring. The use of MDF and chipboard is mainstream in many retail environments.

Steel

Stainless steel, aluminium and powder-coated mild steel are commonly used in the retail environment. Steel can be used structurally, in a shopfront as a glazing frame, as part of the fixture and furniture design, as system upright posts between wall bays, as a decorative cladding to walls or as part of the signage construction.

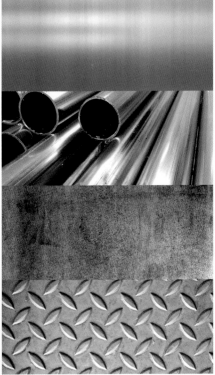

The retail environment Materials

Glass

Glass is incredibly diverse and structurally strong. The retail customer's first experience of the interior and product is through the glazed shopfront window. This glass is laminated (layered bonded glass) for strength and safety. Glass is used for shelving, cabinet displays and sometimes screens. Glass can be coloured using a gel, textured or frosted. Glass can be recycled.

Laminate

Laminates are constructed by layering and fusing kraft or printed papers and resins, with a decorative layer on top, coated in melamine. They are hardwearing and often used as surfaces for counters, wall and door finishes as well as floor finishes mimicking timber. Laminates can be decorative and can be used in innovative ways to create feature walls and displays. They are easy to clean and are durable.

Vinyl and rubber

Vinyl flooring comes in sheet form or tiles in a variety of colours and finishes. It is used in sheet form mainly in the back of house area of the store and ancillary areas, as it is relatively cheap and hardwearing. Vinyl tiles are available in a range of finishes and can imitate timber or stone.

Rubber, like vinyl, comes in sheet and tile formats but can be expensive. It comes in a range of exciting colours and, when sealed, can be water resistant.

Textiles

Different types of textiles are used widely in retail design, from upholstery and fitting room curtains to carpets. Sometimes, the retail designer will work with an upholsterer to custom-clad pieces of furniture. Leather and specialist upholstery fabric are most commonly used. Carpets are sometimes specified for retail environments and can be produced to a specific design or pattern. They come in a variety of finishes, either in man-made or natural fibres. Carpets tend to wear out quickly with heavy traffic and need replacing on a regular basis.

The retail environment Materials

Concrete, terrazzo, quartz

These hard-wearing materials are used predominantly for floor finishes, but sometimes as a wall cladding. Concrete can be polished to give it sheen, coloured with a pigment or moulded to a form of texture, making it very versatile. Concrete, once refined into terrazzo, can be mixed with aggregates such as marble or granite to create a conglomerate, which means that different stones are mixed together. Some conglomerates have quartz added for sparkle. Concrete can be ground down and recycled but this process creates harmful emissions.

Stone, slate and marble

These are traditional, natural materials that can be mixed with concrete to create a conglomerate, or used on their own for flooring, cladding or surface finish. They are hard wearing and have longevity. Each piece will have its own natural flaws. It is important to mention that some stones such as limestone and sandstone can be very porous and stain easily. Vast amounts of water can be used when quarrying, cutting and polishing the stone, which wastes valuable resources.

Ceramic

Ceramic tiles are hardwearing and a cost-effective choice. They come in a variety of finishes and often mimic the look of real stone. They can be used on the floor, walls or as a mosaic pattern, and are waterproof. The finish can be matt or gloss.

Paints and wallpapers

Walls and ceilings are clad in a specific material, painted or wallpapered. A cladding can easily be from a reclaimed material. Some paints are kinder to the environment in terms of their production and emissions and wallpapers can be made from recycled paper and patterned or textured in a range of ways. Wallpaper is once again fashionable and is now widely used both commercially and residentially.

The retail environment Materials

= **THE TIMBERLAND BOOT
COMPANY, TRADING SPACE
London, UK**

DESIGNER
= **CHECKLAND KINDLEYSIDES**

DATE
= **2005**

Timberland seeks to engage in a positive
and sustainable way with the communities
and places located near to the store.
As such, the 'spirit' of the store evolves
from its context and expresses the
company's desire to belong to its locality.
For this first site, the design evolved from
inventiveness, physically building as little
as possible, developing inexpensive and
effective solutions through recycling.
The building at 1 Fournier Street, London,
was previously a banana warehouse and
this provided one of the key display
concepts for the space. Boots are
displayed in clusters hung from the
ceilings, resembling bunches of bananas.
Box rolling racks unearthed from the
basement have been given a new purpose
as display tables and cardboard boxes
stacked on specially designed racking
have created a stockholding wall at the
rear of the store.

: **NAOMI KLEIN**
Brands are the main source of identity.
The brand fills a vacuum and forms a
kind of armour, taking over the part
once played by political, philosophical
or religious ideas.

The retail environment Lighting

= **SONY ERICSSON FLAGSHIP STORE**

DESIGNER
= **CHECKLAND KINDLEYSIDES**

DATE
= **2006**

In their concept for the first Sony Ericsson store, Checkland Kindleysides created a design scheme using simple architectural lines, curvaceous, organic forms to enable the products to be displayed with clarity and elegance. Contrasting with this, they also created a colour-changing fascia that echoed the brand palette and changed in sequence with the lighting in store.

The retail environment is lit predominantly artificially. Natural daylight is evident through the facade but does not always reach into the depth of the store. Also, natural daylight changes throughout the day in terms of its direction and intensity and is affected by the seasons. Artificial lighting is not subject to these changing conditions and can be controlled in a way that natural lighting cannot. Lighting is used to entice the customer into the store and pinpoints the products on display.

Artificial lighting has improved significantly since the light bulb was designed and most people are now conscious of the impact that it has on energy consumption (lighting currently accounts for 40 per cent of energy consumption of non-residential buildings). New lamp technology has given lighting energy-saving efficiency, with LEDs, new CDM-T lamps and fluorescent fittings now in widespread use.

The brightness of artificial lighting is measured in Lux. The brighter the light source, the less energy efficient it becomes. Retail spaces are known for using high levels of Lux, so in recent years research has been conducted to find out the range in which the human eye perceives differences in light levels. In doing this, retailers have lowered the Lux levels without affecting the overall brightness of the interior. For example, the window display, which used to be 1000 Lux, is the brightest element of the store. This has now changed to 750 Lux following these studies, thus decreasing its environmental impact.

The retail designer works closely with a lighting designer to create the desired effect for the branded interior. A reflected ceiling plan is drawn to indicate the positioning of light fittings in relation to the displays, products and services. This drawing is really important in terms of setting out the interior space and will contain a key that identifies all of the light fittings as symbols plotted on to the drawing. Fixtures and fittings are often shown in a dotted line or in a grey or fine line so that the fitting can be lined up correctly with what is happening below. Ceiling features and rafts will also be indicated.

: DAN HEAP
Attention to detail is always at the heart of our lighting design philosophy. By designing the lighting 'into' the building, we ensure it functions and integrates perfectly.

The retail environment Lighting

= **WILLIAM & SONS**
  FLAGSHIP STORE
  London, UK

  DESIGNER
= **SHED DESIGN**

  DATE
= **2008**

  A central raft that runs
  through the length of the
  store enhances the ceiling.
  The detail shows that
  fluorescent light fittings
  are hidden around the
  perimeter of the raft to
  give an even glow.

Principles of lighting

Retail interiors are lit in a very specific
way so that the product is illuminated
to the best advantage and so that the
journey around the store is highlighted
with different layers of brightness and
focus. There are usually three different
layers of light. First is accent lighting,
which highlights the product and is the
brightest element in the store. Second
is task lighting, which is present in the
service areas such as the cash desks,
fitting rooms or consultation spaces
and is not as bright as the accent
lighting. Third is ambient lighting,
which guides the customer around
the walkways and does not impact on
the lighting of the product or services.

Accent lighting

The shop window plays with the
contrast of daylight and artificial light.
As the time or season changes, daylight
fades and gives way to the artificial
illumination. As the customer
approaches the store, the window
display is strongly lit to focus the eye
and draw the customer in. Once inside
the store, the accent lighting is focused
on the product using a variety of fittings
and techniques. Downlighters in the
ceiling wash walls and mid-floor
fixtures, and lighting glows internally
from LEDs in cabinets, creating
lightboxes behind signage.

Lux
The unit by which the brightness of light is measured.

Task and feature lighting

The task lighting illuminates cash desks, fitting rooms, seated areas and consultation spaces. The lighting level is dropped slightly so that it does not interfere with the accent lighting, but is bright enough for the customer and staff to see what they are doing. The task lighting may be in the form of a feature light; a pendant or chandelier to highlight the activity below.

Ambient lighting

The ambient lighting's task is to highlight walkways and give a general glow to the space that does not encroach on the accent or task lighting. The lighting over walkways may be recessed into the ceiling or a row of equally spaced pendants. Often the ambient lighting is incorporated into a ceiling feature, such as a lighting trough, for instance.

= **SELFRIDGES
London, UK**

DATE
= **2006**

This feature lighting runs around the perimeter of the wall and acts as accent lighting, illuminating the products below.

The retail environment Lighting

= **THE WHITE COMPANY**
Brent Cross, UK

DESIGNER
= **CAULDER MOORE**

DATE
= **2006**

This design incorporates a recessed ceiling trough with feature lighting.

= **MAMAS & PAPAS**
Westfield, UK

DESIGNER
= **FOUR IV**

DATE
= **2008**

This feature chandelier hangs through the central circulation void of the store and creates an eye-catching feature.

Light fittings

CDM (CERAMIC DICHARGE METAL HALIDE): This light fitting is incredibly bright and is used in window displays and to wash walls filled with products.

LED (LIGHT EMITTING DIODE): Suitable for cabinet lighting and sometimes used as ambient floor lighting, this fitting has a very low heat emission and is energy efficient. The fitting is made up of a series of small bulbs that are very long lasting and can come in a variety of colours.

LOW-VOLTAGE DOWNLIGHTERS: Low-voltage fittings are used in recessed downlighters. They are used either independently or as secondary lighting for products and can also be used to wash the interior with ambient light. These fittings should be set at about 750mm apart to give an even glow.

FLUORESCENT: These fittings are very versatile and come in a range of lengths between 300mm and 1500mm long. They can also be circular and come small enough to fit inside cabinets. They can be positioned behind ceiling rafts or wall pelmets, overlapping each other for an even glow of ambient light, or using in back-of-house areas as they are inexpensive and efficient. They have an average lifespan of 12,000–20,000 hours.

TRACK LIGHTING: This is often used when there is little or no ceiling void available to recess a light fitting. They are not the most attractive form of lighting, but are efficient in certain circumstances. They come in a range of contemporary styles.

The retail environment Climate and sound

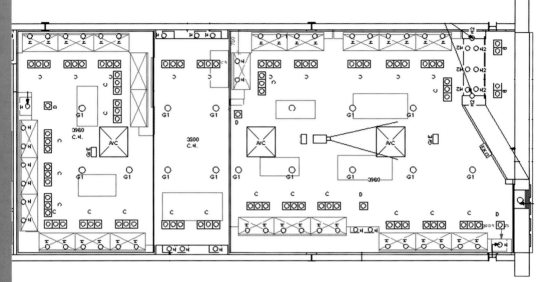

= **A TYPICAL CEILING PLAN
INDICATING SERVICES**

This drawing shows a typical
reflected ceiling plan for
retail. The drawing contains
information about light fittings
and how they are positioned
in relation to the fixtures, and
also shows where the air
conditioning units will sit
within the ceiling and their
relationship to each other,
as they are evenly spaced.

The atmosphere of the interior space can be enhanced or let down by factors that may seem beyond our control, but they are essentially another design consideration in the whole interior scheme. As with all interior projects, designing a space for retail focuses on the customer or user and their comfort within the space. The temperature in the store, as well as the sounds in the store, become part of the ambience and therefore the overall experience. Decisions are clearly made when selecting materials regarding their acoustic qualities and how that will impact on the feel of the space. Climate control is a necessary part of the services required in retail space and sees the merger of skills between the retail designer and a mechanical engineer in resolving these issues.

Air quality

The temperature of an interior space can affect the overall shopping experience and also, of course, the working environment for staff. Retail designers work closely with mechanical engineers specialising in air-conditioning to meet the approved heating and cooling regulations. Once the interior has been proposed, the drawings are passed to the mechanical engineer who then designs the climate control scheme.

The air-conditioning system will consist of ceiling- or wall-mounted air-conditioning units evenly spaced throughout the store and a warm air curtain over the door to relieve the cold draughts coming in from the entrance, which might be permanently open. Each air-conditioning unit is connected to a condenser (most commonly positioned outside), which pulls fresh air through to the air-conditioning unit inside and back again. The connectors are hidden from view in the ceiling void. The mechanical engineer will also include extraction from a kitchen area in the case of a café or restaurant and provide ventilation for toilet facilities.

The retail environment Climate and sound

= **WHITE COMPANY STORE**
Brent Cross, UK

DESIGNER
= **CAULDER MOORE**

DATE
= **2006**

Using a tiled floor and gloss finishes on
the walls in this store enhances the sounds
of the space and will create echoes of
footsteps and conversations, enhancing
the acoustic qualities of the space.

Acoustics

Retail spaces, in most cases, do not have to deal with eliminating high levels of noise from inside the space or from the outside leaking in, and can use the simplest forms of acoustic control to enhance the environment. The shopfront acts as a barrier from the exterior to the interior against street noise. The construction of the interior shell will create an acoustic barrier between retail units; in some instances it may be necessary to use an acoustic grade material between the skin of the wall and stud partition. The main area for concern is in the material finish. Hard materials such as stone, concrete or ceramic floors can be noisy underfoot and would create echoes in a lively store. Some of this noise can add to the ambience of the space. In contrast, soft floor finishes such as carpet deaden sound and may need to be considered for more quiet, private areas such as consultation space or in a book store. Materials cladding the walls can also be used as a barrier for sound; sound-reflecting materials can be used to push sound in a particular direction.

: PETER ZUMTHOR
Listen! Interiors are like large instruments, collecting sound, amplifying it, transmitting it elsewhere.

Acoustics

This describes the scientific study of sound. In terms of the interior, sound can be controlled through the use of materials. Hard materials will bounce sound around a space, creating echoes, while soft materials will absorb sound, creating a quieter space.

The retail environment Student case study

PROJECT
= **TEA HOUSE**

DESIGNER
= **CAROLINE HART**

DATE
= **2008**

= Exterior drawing (above) and
interior drawing (below).

! The intention of this project was to
create a new concept for a Japanese
Tea House on London's wealthy Kings
Road. The resulting design encapsulates
the values of the traditions of the tea
ceremony and looks to incorporate a
retail space, a tea bar, a mini tasting area
on the ground floor and a classroom in
the basement. The journey through the
space is important and is influenced by
age-old rituals and rites of passage.
The client was concerned with ethical
trading and using sustainable materials
where possible to create the overall
interior scheme.

The final design concentrated on colour,
materiality, light and pattern. The design
centred around three uniquely different
spaces, each with its own material and
light quality. Each of the spaces indicated
a different function. The voids between
these different environments also played a
role in the transition between spaces.
Research was carried out to find locally
sourced materials and to consider the
'cradle-to-cradle' approach to recycling.

? Imagine you are working on a
real project and are responsible
for advising both your client and
contractors, as well as specifying
materials.

1 What systems would you put in
place to ensure the comfort of
both staff and customers within
the interior?

2 How would you approach the
lighting scheme? How do you
highlight the product effectively?

3 What materials could you use to
create a particular acoustic
quality?

4 How could you reduce the energy
consumption of a retail space?

= Plans and sections.

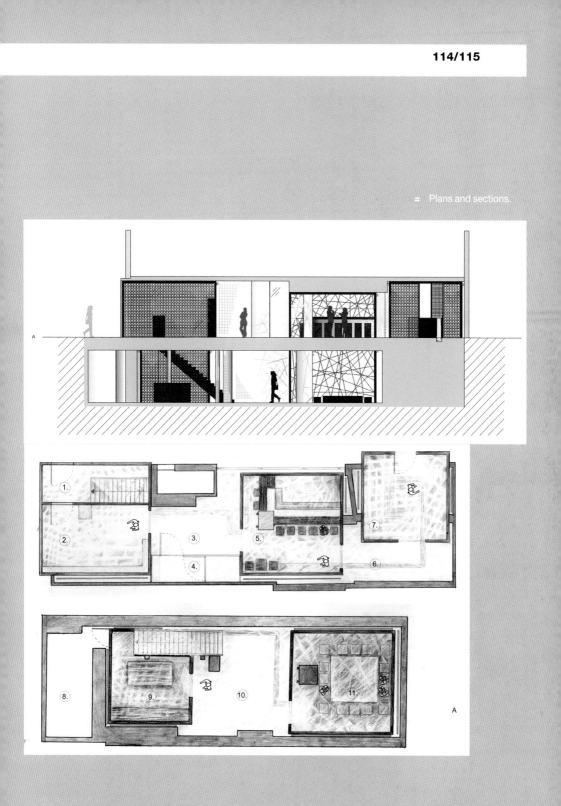

The success of any retail interior does not depend on brand, product or building alone. The interior layout plays an important role in making the transition for the customer from outside to inside seamless. The organisation of the space, from the entrance to the way people navigate and use the area is governed by the layout. This should not encroach on the users; it should not become a conscious part of the overall shopping experience but rather should enhance the quality of the space and the time spent within it.

THIS CHAPTER explores the principles of organising retail space and gives an insight into the techniques used to create an effective, user-friendly layout.

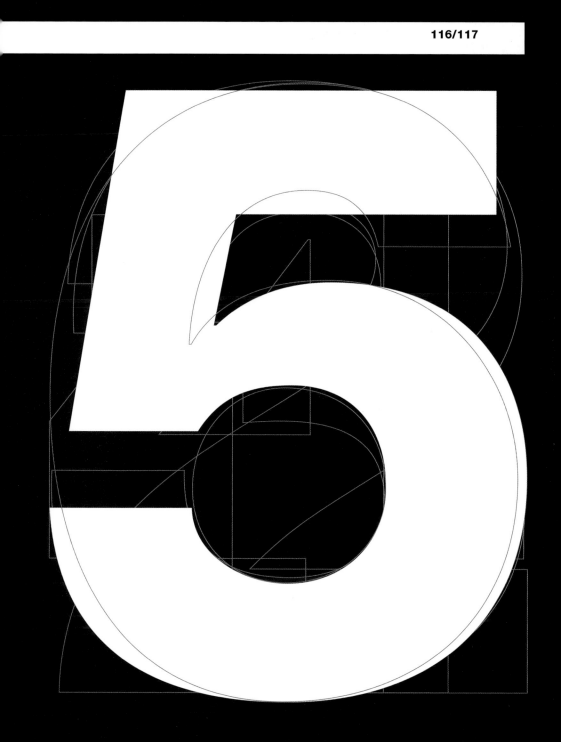

Methods of organising space Principles of retail organisation

= **ORANGE FLAGSHIP STORE**
Rotterdam, Netherlands

DESIGNER
= **QUA**

DATE
= **2005**

The entrance to the Orange store is spacious and inviting, allowing for easy access and a state of transition from the outside to the inside.

Once the brand has been established and the market for its products is fully understood, an analysis of the retailer's current building stock or an investigation into finding a suitable site begins. The brand guidelines for the interior demonstrate a typical size of store for the implementation of the scheme. Although these guidelines set out the rules of layout, they are intended to be adjusted on a site-by-site basis to suit the building (considering its location as well as the interior structure) but the principles within the guide will remain.

The retail designer must also work within the guidelines of building regulations to make sure that the space is accessible to pushchair and wheelchair users and people with other disabilities. The trick is to make these necessary considerations appear seamless and incorporated into the overall scheme as part of the design rather than as an addition.

The overall principles of the interior layout can be broken down into four areas: the entrance, main circulation, pace and finally sales in the form of displays, fixtures and payment areas.

Entrance

The design of the entrance to a store is very important. It needs to entice the customer in and give a glimpse of the products beyond the threshold. The design of the shopfront is discussed in more detail in Chapter 6. In general though, it will be either a new element – fitted as part of the overall scheme – or an existing element preserved in its original form or updated to meet building and planning regulations. Window displays are regularly updated to show the latest products in store. Often, the customer will also be able to see past the window diplays to the store beyond, allowing transparency and interaction. Sometimes the view is blocked by displays, giving a feeling of mystery and bringing the customer's focus to the display.

Once beyond the threshold, the entrance space is the starting point of the interior journey. It is an area of the store that is often left open and spacious, giving the customer time to pause and take in the store environment and to make way for people entering and exiting the store comfortably. In larger stores, it is a place to meet friends before or after shopping, sometimes with seating areas on the sides out of the main flow of traffic.

Signage is an important element of the entrance, used to navigate customers to a correct department or to clearly signpost shop amenities. Lifestyle graphics are also featured in the windows and entrance for brand enhancement.

The entrance is a key main area for featuring new in-store merchandise. This could be in the form of a feature display, or a promotional event including food tasting, free samples, make-overs or sprays of perfume, for example.

The design of the entrance also has to consider access for all users. The entrance must be wide enough for wheelchair and pushchair users and easy for them to manoeuvre. In an existing site, the entrance may be stepped and a ramp may need to encroach into the interior, thus taking a large amount of space from the overall scheme.

: RODNEY FITCH
All the devices of the facade are preludes to the entrance itself ... there should be some sense of transition from the public world outside to the special world of the retailer inside.

Circulation

One of the first tasks the retail designer faces when the site has been decided is to work out the circulation around the space, taking into consideration the design guidelines and principles of the scheme alongside the structural nature of the interior. Circulation diagrams are produced as ways of thinking and describing different schemes to the client. The diagrams are produced by looking at the plans and sections of the interior and drawing arrows and routes over the technical drawings. The circulation plan is often drawn in unison with an adjacency plan (often on the same drawing), which shows how the areas of the space will be divided into product, places to sell, space to browse and ancillary areas. These drawings form the starting point for planning the interior layout.

The circulation performs two main tasks in the retail scheme. The first is to allow for the flow of people in the form of walkways. These must be wide enough for at least two people to pass each other comfortably, whether walking or in a wheelchair, or pushing a pram. The second is to take the customer to the merchandise and allow them ample space to browse without bumping into other people or displays.

The principles of circulation are quite simple and are governed by the ways in which people move around the space. There are many ways that this can happen but each is based around a handful of solutions. Circulation can work horizontally, allowing the customer access through the shopfront, with products displayed either side of the walkway and with an exit at the back; or vertically, with merchandise displayed over more than one floor. This scheme is more complicated in the sense that stairs, lifts and escalators need to be negotiated, and methods for enticing people on to the upper floors must be considered. Circulation in a zig-zag or figure-of-eight fashion across the store allows for points of interest to be included and creates a longer journey and a variety of ways to travel around the space. The circular pattern takes customers from the front to the back and then to the front again.

Circulation
A controlled route that users take around a building.

Pace

Pace is an interesting aspect of circulation design that analyses how people use the space as well as move around it. Pace is very much influenced by the nature of the user and their lifestyle, which is one reason why it is important to understand the market targeted by the brand and the area in which the store will be located. The coffee shop concept is a good example for describing how pace plays a part in the overall plan of the interior as it often considers many paces within the scheme and is marketed at many different types of user groups. The paces described are fast, medium and slow. The fast-paced user will want to buy a take-away coffee and exit the shop immediately. This is why most large chain coffee shops have a service counter that works very much like a production line. The aim is to keep the customers moving as much as possible to give the impression of quick service. Also, coffee shops have a high volume of customers, which suits this type of service. The medium-paced user will go through this service process, then they will sit in the shop to drink and eat their purchase. They might stay for a maximum time of 20 minutes.

This seating area is usually located at the front of the shop, in the form of high stools at the windows or on chairs around small tables. This allows the user to get back outside when finished without having to move through the whole shop. The slow-paced user purchases food and drink and sits for a longer period, often on comfortable chairs and sofas with access to newspapers. These users may stay for an hour or so to meet friends or have their lunch break at a comfortable setting away from the frenetic service area. Also, in some coffee shops an area is put aside for business meetings, offering a quiet space at the back of the shop with a boardroom-like table with up to eight seats around it.

In smaller retail stores, pace is not an issue, but larger stores such as department stores consider the nature of the users and provide a number of entrances and exits for a quick visit as well as a more meandering experience.

Pace
The speed at which someone moves around a space. Retail designers often consider a range of paces when designing an interior scheme.

Methods of organising space Principles of retail organisation

= **LAFAYETTE MAISON**
Paris, France

DESIGNER
= **SAGUEZ & PARTNERS**

DATE
= **2004**

Lafayette Maison houses the home store department within one of the largest department stores in the world, Lafayette. The store is laid out so that the products on each floor correspond with a room in a house. The basement is the kitchen, selling cookware and utensils, the ground floor is the entrance hall where visitors are welcomed in the large foyer, the first floor is the dining room containing dining furniture, the second floor is the living room, stocking essential lounge items and the third floor houses the bedroom and bathroom ranges.

Signage played an important role in the overall design. The designers needed to ensure that the layout was easy to navigate, enabling the customer to wander around and discover other areas of the store without getting lost.

The atrium is the central focus, with horizontal movement around the periphery and open views through all windows. The tills and service desks always remain in the same position and furniture displays are arranged so as not to interrupt views through the building.

Methods of organising space Principles of retail organisation

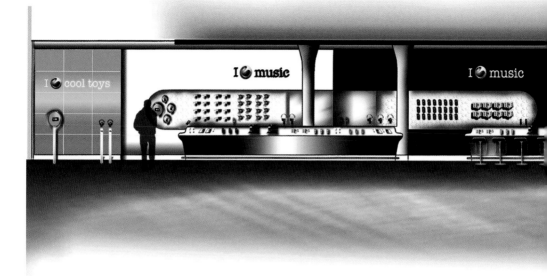

Sales

The most important thing about any retail interior is its ability to sell products and sustain the business. The entrance, circulation and pace are all important design issues for the retail designer to contend with, but it is the products and the way in which they are displayed that is the biggest challenge. It is important to mention that although it is the most essential area for development within the scheme, it would not function without the other areas we have already considered.

= **SONY ERICSSON
FLAGSHIP STORE**

DESIGNER
= **CHECKLAND KINDLEYSIDES**

DATE
= **2006**

This scheme shows the development of Sony Ericsson's first dedicated store, which coincided with their fifth anniversary and the launch of their brand treatment. The aim of the store was to reflect the new direction of the brand by creating an engaging environment and to encourage a much broader range of consumers. The look is cool and contemporary. The images show the development of the layout including adjacency planning of the products and the consideration of circulation. The graphics clearly signpost the product types. Merchandise is displayed in a way that does not interrupt the circulation flow.

Methods of organising space Merchandising

Understanding the product and the necessary quantities needed on display and in immediate storage is paramount to successful merchandising. Retailers' stock tends to change on a regular basis, so flexibility is the key to a functional display fixture. The positioning of merchandise within the interior is very important. Retailers understand their key products and what draws their customers in. The retail designer must use this wealth of knowledge and experience to arrange the products throughout the store so that the customer is enticed from one to another on a particular journey.

In the design manual, the retailer's merchandising principles are set out as part of the branding and marketing agenda. The retailer may have very specific requirements depending on the merchandise and the range of other related products. For instance, it may be important to always have four wall bays in a row without a break with shelves above. Most large retailers have an in-house merchandising team who spend their time working with the products in a generic space (usually in the retailer's main branch office) and deriving solutions to displaying the items effectively. Many products work in collections. Fashion and clothing is a good example of this, where the clothes and related accessories need to be displayed together.

= **LULU GUINNESS BOUTIQUE**
London, UK

DESIGNER
= **HMKM**

DATE
= **2009**

In order to elevate the existing Sloane Street Lulu Guinness flagship store to a luxury boutique, HMKM created a concept that would reflect the high quality of the merchandise on display. They achieved this using silver-leafed wall panels, Swarovski crystal-encrusted wallpaper, plaster-moulded mirrors and marble-topped display tables. HMKM's resulting design demonstrates a thorough knowledge and understanding of the merchandise being offered for sale.

Methods of organising space Merchandising

Product display

Taking up a large part of the retail designer's remit is the design of fixture displays. Some fixtures can be bought in a kit form and either used directly in this state, or adjusted with finishes to suit the interior design; other fixtures are custom made. Custom-made pieces work particularly well if the scheme is to be rolled out; the cost of making the fixtures becomes cheaper with larger production quantities. For one-off stores, an off-the-shelf system may be a better solution. These elements, although not at the forefront of the consumer's experience, are the vehicles that drive the interior scheme and make the space function and sell products. Products can be displayed in a variety of interesting ways, but can be broken down into two different types: wall display and mid-floor fixtures.

Using the interior walls is one of the main ways to display products. Go into most retail spaces and the walls will be lined from floor to ceiling with goods. The only instance where this may not be seen is in the premium retail sector as smaller amounts of product are displayed to give a feeling of exclusivity. The principle of the design of the wall fixture is simple. They tend to be (and should have the ability to be) constructed from panels so that they can hold an array of hooks and hangers that can be adjusted to suit any situation. The retail designer will make the wall fixtures unique to the scheme through its material finish. The wall allows for a high level of stock over a large surface, which frees up the central spaces for circulation and feature displays. Between the standard bays are opportunities to make feature statements through specialist display and graphics.

The mid-floor fixtures consist of a selection of different elements that create interest and stagger the customer's view so that glimpses of stock behind can be seen. The fixtures could be in the form of tables, cabinets or free-standing gondolas, or could be wrapped around a column, for instance.

: WILLIAM GREEN
Display areas are at the heart of a retail store. Display is the mechanism that presents the merchandise to the shopper in its most favourable light and that permits the shopper to evaluate and select products for purchase.

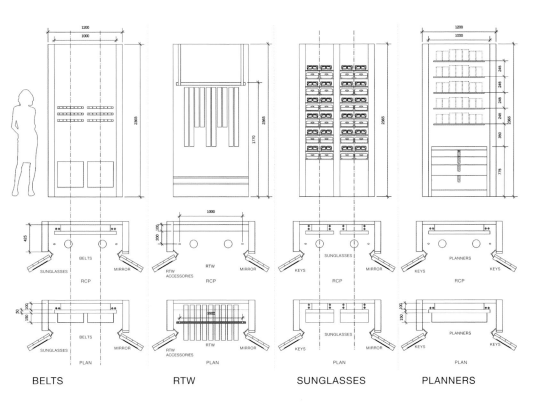

BELTS   RTW   SUNGLASSES   PLANNERS

= **MULBERRY**
Various locations

DESIGNER
= **FOUR IV**

DATE
= **2008**
This is a sheet of technical drawings showing the variations of wall 'wardrobe' displays for Mulberry stores.

Methods of organising space Service and ancillary space

As well as displaying products, the retail space must include areas for customer service. For most, this will happen at the point of sale when goods are being purchased. But there will also be dedicated space at which customer/staff contact can mean a sale.

These spaces consist of fitting rooms and staff/customer consultation areas. These are support areas, and although used for selling, they do not necessarily contain displayed stock. The design of these spaces is just as important as that of the main displays. Because they are used by the public they are carefully considered in order that they work alongside the branded interior in terms of finish and graphics, and so that they convey a positive image of the customer service.

The ancillary space refers to the area that is put aside to house the functional elements of the store, aside from selling. This area supports the running and managing of the store on a daily basis and provides essential areas for storage and facilities for staff and is often referred to as 'back of house'. Public toilets are often provided in larger retail stores and come under the heading of 'ancillary'.

= **SELFRIDGES FITTING ROOMS**
London, UK

DATE
= **2006**

The design of the fitting rooms in
this image coincides with that of
the store so that the shopping
experience continues.

Methods of organising space Service and ancillary space

Fitting rooms

In fashion stores, fitting rooms are essential for customers to 'try before they buy'. There have been some trends in fitting room design over the years that are worth mentioning. High street fashion stores once favoured one big open space for all with mirrors all around. Some stores also had a small amount of very tight cubicles with badly fitted curtains alongside the open space, making the trying on of clothes an uncomfortable experience for many. Most now have separate spacious cubicles for changing with mirrors on all sides, a fixed seat, hooks for your own clothes and bags and a solid lockable door for added discretion.

The entrance into the fitting room can be a key area to enhance the shopping experience. In larger stores, this space contains seating and sometimes even entertainment for those who have to wait. In smaller stores that do not have the space to do this, the most basic entrance will have a rail for unwanted items and sometimes a sales assistant to help and log the clothes that are being tried on (fitting rooms are one of the main places where shoplifting occurs).

: **SAGUEZ & PARTNERS**
... you need to catch your breath, need a meeting point, somewhere to sit down, to take a break... and clean toilets where you can redo your makeup, a left-luggage facility to leave your packages while you carry on shopping, refreshment areas, a car park, a deliveries area ...

Another aspect of fitting room design that is notoriously important is lighting. The positioning of the light fitting in relation to the mirror and the colour of the light shining on to bare skin can be unflattering and would not aid a sale. As technology has progressed, fitting room lighting has taken a different approach with many cubicles containing a switch so that the customer can adjust the lighting levels and colour to suit.

Every clothing store must have a fitting room equipped for customers with disabilities. The room must be large enough to take a wheelchair; it must have grab rails and a strategically placed mirror as well as a seat. In very small stores, it is acceptable to have just one changing cubicle, but it must comply with disability rights and laws and building regulations.

Consultation areas

For the majority of retailers, customer service is key to consumer enjoyment. In the mobile phone, jewellery and now eyewear sectors, as well as showrooms for cars, furniture and white goods, consultation areas or booths are an integral part of the interior scheme. These are spaces where a customer can sit with a salesperson and discuss their purchase needs. The area often consists of a table of some sort with seats positioned so that two customers can sit opposite the salesperson. Some consultation areas are private so that the customer feels at ease with an expensive purchase, or public, demonstrating to other customers that transactions take place. When designing consultation areas, the designer has to be aware of the customer's needs: private or public, noisy or quiet, so that the correct furniture and screening can be used. Also, the consultation desk will need to house equipment so that transactions can take place.

= **PORSCHE SHOWROOM**
Leusden, Netherlands

DESIGNER
= **QUA**

DATE
= **2004**

This sketch of a consultation area for a car showroom shows a typical layout with three seats, one for the salesperson opposite the customers.

Methods of organising space   Service and ancillary space

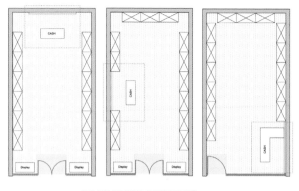

= CASH DESK POSITION

These drawings depict the various positions of the cash desk and how they sit alongside the merchandise and work with the circulation. The design of the cash desk coincides with the overall design scheme. It is often well lit and easy to see from all around the store.

Point of sale

The point of sale marks the end of the journey around the store and is the point at which a customer will pay for goods. The location of the point of sale is very important. In larger stores, there will be access to till points in several locations, often relating to a department, one in menswear and one in womenswear, for example. In supermarkets, the till points are usually located in front of the exit doors. This allows for heavy traffic flow in a runway fashion and indicates the end of the overall process. In smaller stores, the till point or cash desk can be located in a number of places: at the back of the store, with a feature wall behind it so that it can be seen from the shopfront; halfway into the store along a side wall, dividing the product display; or at the front of the store, close to the entrance and marking the end of the shopping experience. Also, positioning the till point by the entrance of a small store where there may only be one or two members of staff working is advantageous. The entrance/exit can be watched by the staff from the till to deter shoplifters. In some retail instances, the point of sale may be a self-service coin/card machine. These devices are increasingly being used in supermarkets, petrol stations and train stations to provide a quicker service at peak times.

As well as being a place to pay for goods, the point of sale also holds a merchandising opportunity with 'impulse' buys such as chocolate, stamps or phone top-ups.

= **SELFRIDGES CASH DESK**
London, UK

DATE
= **2006**

This stylish cash desk sits in front of a feature wall and is internally lit, clearly demonstrating its use with graphics.

Methods of organising space Service and ancillary space

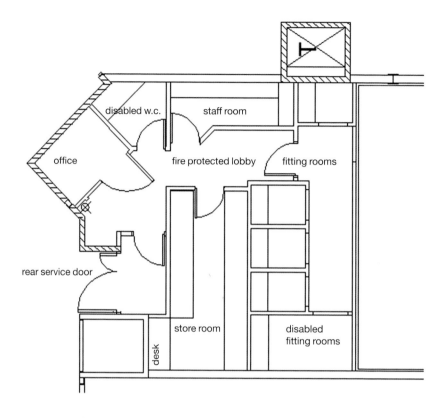

disabled w.c.

staff room

office

fire protected lobby

fitting rooms

rear service door

store room

disabled fitting rooms

desk

= A TYPICAL BACK-OF-HOUSE PLAN

This drawing shows a typical back-of-house plan.

Back of house

The 'back-of-house' area is the part of the store that the customer never sees. As its name suggests, it is almost always positioned at the back of the store. This is so that it is located off the service area behind the shop unit for easy access for deliveries and removing packaging and other waste from site. There is often a door that leads directly to the service area from the back of the store so that deliveries aren't taken through the main shop. This door can also act as a secondary fire escape from the building and it is important to make sure that the hallway from the store to the rear exit is wide and without obstacles.

Within the back-of-house area there will be, at the least, a staff room containing a basic kitchen with microwave, kettle and table and chairs, staff toilets (this could be one disabled cubicle for small stores, or a separate male and female facility), a small manager's office and a stockroom. The stockroom will be as large as possible and racked up to the ceiling, usually using a standard storage kit, some of which come with mezzanine constructions to take full advantage of the height of the space. The finish to the 'back-of-house area' is basic but durable, using cost-effective materials throughout.

Customer toilets

In department stores and supermarkets, the provision of customer toilet facilities is essential, especially if the store contains eating or refreshment facilities. Some treat these areas like back of house with basic fittings and finishes, whilst others choose to continue the branding into the toilets. The design and choice of cubicle partitions and sanitary ware, as well as floor and wall finishes, depend on their durability and easiness to clean as they are very well used and are sometimes subject to vandalism. If customer toilets are offered, then facilities for disabled customers must also be provided.

Methods of organising space Student case study

PROJECT
= CHÉM DOL SOFIA

DESIGNER
= KATIE DRAKE-BURROWS

DATE
= 2005

! This project sees the division of space into a series of 'haute couture' parlour and event areas that have been designed to inform the consumer of latest fashions. The space consists of three activities: exhibition, retail, bar and restaurant.

The existing building that was to house this fashion experience has seen many structural changes through its life, with different retailers taking ownership of the space and dividing it up. The main challenge of this project was to investigate the building's structure and to manipulate it to suit the new circulation, which became paramount to the store design. The central space was opened up to create a main atrium and circulation space through all floors, which is reminiscent of department store layouts (see Chapter 3). This allowed for an easy transition between each area both vertically and horizontally.

The retail area is laid out using the principles of organising retail space. The walls are used effectively to display racks of shoes and clothing in neat arrangements, telling the story of each collection, with feature areas in between. Elegant free-standing wardrobes and tree-like fixtures bring the product into the centre of each space, leaving wide circulation space around each object and creating effectively lit features. Cash areas are strategically placed in each section and fitting rooms are tucked into the corners. There is also space to sit and linger, challenging the customer to engage in the shopping experience and adding quality to the customer service.

? Imagine you are producing a layout for a retail scheme.

1 What journey do you want the customer to take around the space?

2 How will you position products in relation to each other?

3 What features would you use to draw the customer through the store?

4 What types of service space do you need and how does their positioning relate to the product?

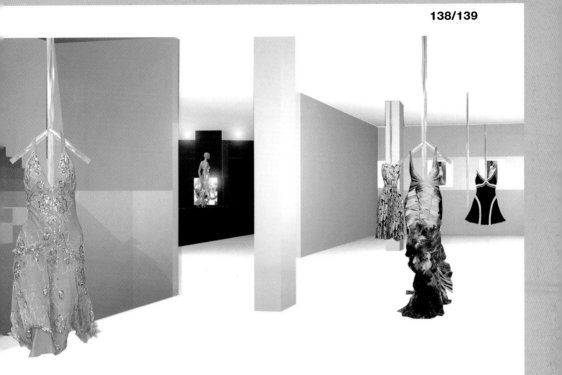

= Image showing the exhibition space in the basement.

= Image showing the fitting rooms.

= Image showing the entrance with directional signage.

= Plan showing the circulation around the main retail space.

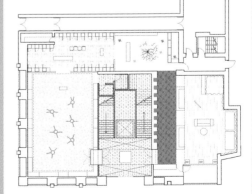

The final stage of designing for retail is in the detail. Every component in the overall scheme is developed alongside the brand.

THIS CHAPTER examines the considerations that need to be made: the architecture of each building or site; the role of the shopfront and how its configuration and style impacts on the interior scheme; the interior structure and the elements of the design scheme that work within it in the form of walls, ceilings and floor finishes, and the fixtures, fittings and components.

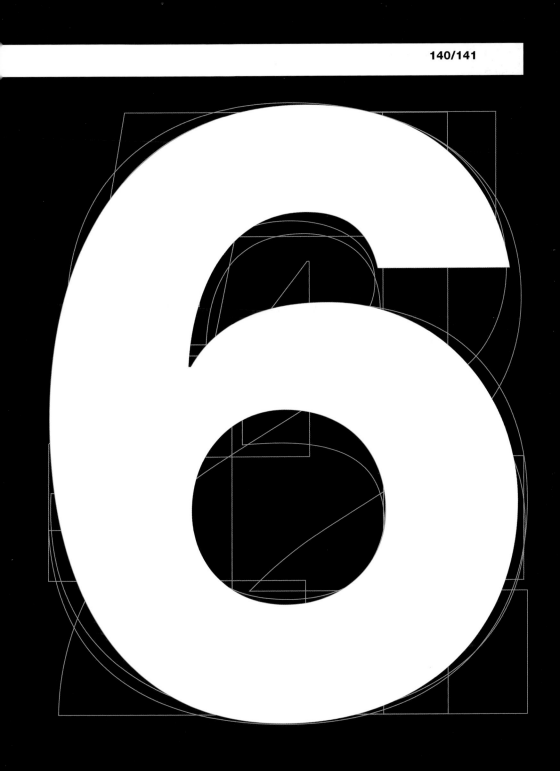

Design detail The shop façade

The shopfront's main task is to communicate to potential customers the essence of the interior and to display a glimpse of what can be found on the other side of the glass. In most cases, the shopfront is a draw to buyers to make them feel comfortable when approaching the store and venturing over the threshold. For others, it is an opportunity to window-shop and aspire to buy into the lifestyle on view. In some instances, the shopfront and entrance are designed to deter the public from entering, with security on the door, having to ring a bell at the entrance or needing an appointment to enter. This particular method is used in premium retail where exclusivity and wealth are expected.

: MARCEL WANDERS
... product designers have a tendency to work more on details – to be innovative on the small parts and make things function.

There are many considerations that need to be made when designing a shopfront. The shop facade must first take on the essence of the brand. This is done through graphic communication: fascia signage, a projecting sign, window details and lifestyle graphics as part of the window displays; the materials from which a new shopfront is constructed, or how an existing shopfront can be adapted to meet the design requirements; the merchandise in the window and the brand message that is conveyed by the window display; and the position of the entrance door and how this will be managed.

As part of the interior design manual for the retailer, a variety of shopfront configurations are explored. The approach to shopfront design will vary depending on the site location and the impact of the design of the neighbouring shop facades, as well as planning and listed building requirements. In the case of shopping centres, neighbouring retail outlets and arcades will have to be considered. Also, when a retailer rents a shop unit, a contract is drawn up between the retailer and landlord to outline what can and can't be done to the unit or building. If the shopfront is to be retained, this contract will state the conditions.

Although the design of the shopfront varies from site to site, within the rules of the location guidelines, there are common principles and techniques that are applied. The two main style choices come under the headings of traditional and contemporary; there are obvious design differences under each heading. The principles of entrance, its size and the impact of its positioning on the interior are also important areas of consideration, as is the choice of signage displays.

Design detail The shop façade

The traditional shopfront

The design of the traditional shopfront has a sense of symmetry and is set out in proportion to the existing building's elevation. In most cases, unless the brand's design states it, it is unusual to put a 'new' traditional shopfront into a site unless required to do so for planning reasons or to suit the design scheme of an arcade or shopping centre as a replacement of an existing older shopfront. If this is the case, then restrictions may also be in place regarding the application of signage and the colour in which the shopfront can be painted. In some instances, a standard font, text size and colour may be specified as well as the type of signage. Signage may have to be painted onto the fascia rather than applied on a fascia box, and a standard projecting sign to match all others in the centre may be part of the conditions.

The contemporary shopfront

The design of the contemporary shopfront focuses on allowing light and visual access right into the store from the street. The look is clean, with glazing reaching from floor to fascia panel, or sometimes with the fascia situated inside the glass, sat in a brushed stainless steel frame. Sometimes the glazing is frameless around the internal elements. The signage is influenced by the brand, using contemporary fonts and ways of representing text. Illuminated sign boxes are the normal application in contrast to a traditional painted sign.

= A TRADITIONAL SHOPFRONT

This line drawing reflects the typical qualities of a traditional shopfront, taking its proportions from the existing building's elevation.

= **FULLCIRCLE**
London, UK

DATE
= **2008**

This shopfront has a large opening directly onto the shopping mall, making the transition from the walkway into the store seamless.

Design detail The shop façade

= **VILLANDRY SHOPFRONT**

DESIGNER
= **DALZIEL AND POW**

DATE
= **2007**

This shopfront leads directly on to the street, is constrained by the building's existing architecture and has canopies to shelter customers from the weather.

: SHONQUIS MONERO
A pane of glass... divides the shop from the pavement. On one side, the climate-controlled interior welcomes those who can buy; on the other, the intemperate street is where those who cannot buy may look without paying – in the time-honoured tradition of window-shopping.

Entrance doors

The entrance doors need to be easily accessible to all, so must therefore be at least 1000mm in width. A hinged door must open inwards so not to obstruct the street or path in front and must give good security to the store at night. An alternative to the hinged door is sliding doors that have a cleaner look and do not impact on the interior in any way. In some situations, a roller shutter performs the function of a door.

The position of the entrance door is key to the success of the entrance as a whole. A central doorway allows for symmetry and is therefore visually comfortable. Also, this enables the store to be laid out in a symmetrical fashion so that the focus from the entrance is on the central space, and in some cases, the back wall of the store, providing an opportunity to draw the customer in with a feature. Positioning the door to one side offsets the interior. This may be necessary if there is a particular reason for needing one large window display instead of two smaller ones, or if a cash desk is positioned at the front of the store directly behind the window. It is often the case that the shopfront is inherited from a previous owner and therefore the current retailer has to adapt the scheme to suit the existing entrance position. Replacing a shopfront can be costly and is often an area where costs can be cut if the current structure can be upgraded through decoration.

Internal/external shopfront

The designer faces different design opportunities and solutions depending on whether the store is in an internal setting such as a shopping centre, arcade or retail outlet or if it is directly on the street. The design of the internal shopfront in a mall, for example, does not have to consider weather conditions and so can be of a more open design. The entrance into the unit may have a shutter for security without a solid door behind and may be very wide – some are the width of the entire frontage. Also, the internal shopfront, depending on the guidelines of the shopping centre, will probably have an area in front of the unit called a 'pop-out zone', which is usually about 500–1000mm deep. This means that part of the shopfront design can literally pop out into the mall. This technique is used to create visual differences between shop units and is used when shopping centres want to encourage differentiation in shopfront design.

The external shopfront has to be completely secure and weatherproof and will have solid lockable access, probably with a roller shutter, either just in front of the door or the whole frontage. The shopfront will also have to sit comfortably with its neighbours and possibly the whole row, in order to comply with fascia panel rules and guidelines. This restricts opportunities to play with the design.

Design detail The shop façade

= **THORNTONS**
London, UK

DESIGNER
= **CAULDER MOORE**

DATE
= **2008**

This shopfront allows the customer to view the making process of the products within. The door is off-centre to allow for space for a counter on the left-hand side. The full-height glazing has a coloured vinyl applied to what would be the underside of the counter and window fixture, which enables the product displayed in the window to be raised to a more comfortable viewing level.

The shop window

The shop window begins with a pane of glass that creates a division between the exterior and the interior. In most new shopfronts, the glazing covers as large an area as possible, so much so that the division barely exists. Shop window design is an art and a profession in its own right, with new concepts reaching windows on a cyclical basis.

The purpose of the display is to create a memorable vision and to portray the brand values in one punchy statement. The display must be consistent with the interior and product range in the materials used, the way the display is lit and the graphic communication. The window suggests the lifestyle that can be achieved from owning the products and entices the customer inside. The size of the window display and the way the merchandise is set out must be coherent to the products displayed. For instance, larger items need a spacious window so that the shopper can stand back to look, whilst smaller items need to be displayed at eye level so that the shopper can walk up close and view them without bending or stretching.

Most window displays are designed around a shallow plinth that raises the merchandise to an appropriate height in relation to the glazing, and allows for mannequins, price statements and additional blocks to be added for smaller products. The retailer's merchandising team usually source mannequins, but occasionally the retail designer will advise them.

Some retailers use the window as the main vehicle from which to sell stock. The traditional jeweller's window is a good example of this. The window display extends into the shop, taking up a large proportion of the retail space, leaving the interior for sales and service alone. The display element for jewellery is very detailed as it has the job of holding a variety of pads containing stock filling the whole window.

Facade
The front elevation of a building. In retailing, the facade acts as an advertisement for the store within, displaying signage and large plate glass windows for display purposes.

Shopfront signage

The design of shopfront signage is often governed by the location of the site and any conditions applied by landlords, centre management or planning. There are a variety of options available for each situation. The retail designer will work with a signage manufacturer to come up with suitable solutions. The main signage types are fascia sign, projecting sign and window decals.

The design of the fascia sign may appear varied on the high street, but they commonly fall under one of three types of signage: the traditional painted sign as already discussed; an illuminated box sign that is constructed most commonly in a 'biscuit-tin' formation, constructed from aluminium with the logo or lettering fret cut out of the face and replaced with frosted acrylic (the box contains fluorescent light fittings that are easily accessible by removing the top of the 'biscuit tin') and, finally, a logo or letters that have been fret cut out of a sheet of aluminium or steel (possibly spray painted or brushed) that are then pegged off the fascia panel and often illuminated from an external source.

= **SIZE?**
Bristol, UK

DESIGNER
= **CHECKLAND**
KINDLEYSIDES

DATE
= **2009**

This unique shopfront has a black-and-white photograph applied to the facade. Inspired by its location in The Horsefair, Bristol, the signage of this shopfront thus takes direct reference from the store's locality.

The projecting sign, in a similar fashion, can either be a traditional painted sign or an illuminated box sign (constructed in the same way as the fascia sign) suspended from a steel frame bolted into the shopfront. Some retailers, especially banks and jewellery stores, have clocks projecting from the fascia instead of signage.

Window decals are necessarily applied to meet building regulations. A decal is a graphic made from vinyl that is applied directly to the glass at eye level and is there to stop people from walking through the glass. Most retailers stick to a simple decal that does not detract from the view into the shop and makes the glass look as though it is frosted, whilst others create a graphic statement over the entire window. The vinyl is self-adhesive and can be easily removed.

Design detail Interior architecture

Part of the retail designer's job is to survey the site before producing the drawing package for the implementation of the retail scheme. This may be to check dimensions from drawings that may have already been obtained, or it could be to carry out a full survey so that an existing set of drawings can be produced. Depending on the complexities of the site, it may be preferable to employ an architect or surveyor to undertake this task.

As retail sites tend to change hands frequently, there are often anomalies within the building's structure where major work may need to be done to reconfigure the interior to suit the new scheme. With this in mind, the design solutions are often left open to compromise. This is the challenge facing any interior designer working within an existing building.

It is sometimes possible to retain the architectural details created or maintained by others and working with them is the most environmentally friendly solution. Sometimes, this will not work and, understandably, the site will be stripped out.

In retail, the term 'architecture' refers to the fabric of the building: ceilings, walls and floors. These are all elements that become part of the overall scheme, but in many cases remain a neutral backdrop against which to display the main brand elements. Design trends come and go, but over the past 20 years we have seen changes in retail design so great that they have left a stamp on the architecture of many buildings. First came the 'white box'; a design concept based on an art gallery, using a minimal interior to show clothes off to their full potential. Then came the 'black box' as a reaction to the 'white box'. Then came the introduction of colour, pattern and texture, hand in hand with the evolution of the organic form.

Retail design often plays tricks with the interior space, creating a stage for the performance of the brand, or a façade masking the true architecture of the space.

: **G. BROOKER & S. STONE**
... they are re-modelled, reused, rethought and yet a suggestion of the former meaning disturbs and inspires the subsequent design ...

= **ALL SAINTS**
  Glasgow, UK

DATE
= **2003**

The interior of this retail space strongly
reflects the identity of the All Saints brand.
The design focuses on the rich heritage
features of the site, which was a former
post office, whilst contrasting with the
custom-made lighting and furniture. The
building has been stripped back to reveal
its fabric and structure and has been left,
in places, in its raw state.

Design detail Interior architecture

Ceilings

The ceiling plays a huge role in the feel of the entire retail space. It is the architectural element that goes mostly unnoticed, but it is incredibly functional. Within the ceiling are light fittings, air-conditioning ducts, fire alarms, sometimes sprinklers and music speakers. The general design principles for ceilings can be investigated through three different types: suspended ceilings, ceiling rafts and open ceilings.

The suspended ceiling is constructed from either a timber frame or is suspended from Dexion rods with plasterboard applied and skimmed to the underside. The suspended ceiling leaves a void of 150 – 500mm between the actual ceiling and the false ceiling, providing enough room for all of the functions to be hidden in between. This solution works very well in spaces that have a good ceiling height to start with (so that the ceiling does not become too low) and gives a clean finish to the overall space. Also, sinking in or dropping areas within the ceiling to create opportunities to spill light, gives the feeling of a true architectural feature.

Ceiling rafts are similar to a suspended ceiling in their construction, but they only cover areas of the ceiling space. They are often positioned over specific interior elements to create a design through the volume of the space, or to coincide with functional items hidden within the ceiling. Also, the material from which the raft is constructed may be quite adventurous and unique to the design scheme.

An open ceiling design is one with no suspended elements and the ceiling structure is completely visible along with all of the air conditioning ducts, lighting and wiring etc. If the store has a high ceiling then this design can appear industrial and may suit the requirements of the interior scheme. One way to avert one's gaze from the ceiling, is to paint the ceiling and all of the fittings in black. This concept is taken from theatre design where blacked-out elements focus the viewer's eye on the entertainment. In retail, this masks the unsightly components and concentrates shopper's view on the products. This is an effective solution that is often used in stores that have a lower budget – such as a retail outlet, which in most cases has a high ceiling. When the ceiling is low (this can be found mostly in existing older buildings or in basements), then the ceiling can become problematic. A suspended ceiling cannot be used as there is not enough height, and the low ceiling means that nothing can be recessed or hidden away. Also, the customer's eye level is too close to the ceiling to mask any ceiling functions with dark paint. In this instance, the best possible solution is to keep the ceiling as clear as possible, using the joint between the ceiling and walls to hide cables. Track lighting with wall-mounted fittings is almost the only option for lighting.

= **VERTU STORE**
London, UK

DESIGNER
= **SHED DESIGN**

DATE
= **2007**

This wall feature cleverly holds product, recessed and lit within a black strip. The feature is architecturally interesting and suits the brand concept.

The ceiling feature sits above the central space and highlights the car displayed below. The ceiling 'floats' and a recessed lighting feature appears like a shaft of daylight, spilling into life.

Design detail Interior architecture

Walls

Walls are one of the most important elements in the retail environment. Not only do they support the building structurally, but they can be used to display vast amounts of products, create feature displays and have colour, texture and pattern applied to them in different finishes. Many retail designers use the wall to carry the design concept through the scheme. Walls can act as dividers between product offers or areas, as a piece of sculpture in its own right, or to add focus to a space.

Floors

Floors come in a variety of materials and finishes, but the key to a retail floor is durability. The expected lifespan of a floor finish can be anything from one year to 20 years depending on the retailer's needs. The quality of the floor finish often suggests something about the quality of the merchandise. A cheap floor such as vinyl or carpet will wear out quickly and is often a quick fix, whilst an expensive floor such as granite or marble will have longevity and a sense of luxury.

There are many medium-cost flooring solutions that are durable and interesting in terms of pattern and colour, and work with the overall branded interior. Rubber, timber, ceramic or terrazzo are favourable solutions.

The floor finish is used to define different areas within the store. Walkways, display areas and point of sale may all have different finishes within the same scheme.

Shadow gap
A contemporary detail used to create a junction between walls, ceilings and floors; or between a fixture and the floor, so that the objects displayed on it appear to be floating.

= **CASIO**
London, UK

DATE
= **2005**

This was the first Casio brand store implemented in the UK, bringing together all of the Casio sub-brands in a unique 'Casiology' environment. The site, on London's Carnaby Street, underwent a total transformation inside and outside, using graphics and imagery from the current 'Casiology' advertising campaign. Solid black imagery of leaves, flowers and butterflies wraps right around the walls and across the floor, creating movement and fluidity as customers enter the store. Passersby are drawn in by the layered imagery also used on the windows, and Casio-blue mirrored glass display plinths with thick faceted glass tops display merchandise. Simple but effective lighting is hidden within slots in the ceiling, creating a glow both day and night, the total effect reinforcing the brand's timelessness and quality in a fresh aspirational way.

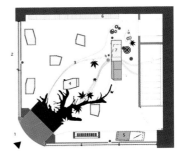

Design detail Fixtures and fittings

= **MARNI STORE**
London, UK

DESIGNER
= **FUTURE SYSTEMS**

DATE
= **1999**

Future Systems were invited to
create a concept for all Marni
stand-alone shops and units
within department stores in
London, Milan, Paris, New York,
Tokyo and Kuwait. The store
concept was generated by the
textures, colour, composition
and beauty of the clothes
themselves, which were
presented on sculptural islands,
sitting against the brightly
coloured backdrop of the shop.

The fixtures and fittings are the details that make up the functional elements of the store's interior. The design of such fixtures sees the retail designer taking on a role very similar to that of a furniture designer, who in most cases is designing furniture or display fixtures for mass-production. Each fixture is designed down to the last detail, specifying all materials through to fastenings. In some cases, off-the-shelf fixtures can be used or adapted to suit, and this may be an advantageous approach for small retailers, but for roll-out and premium retail, the bespoke piece can be cost-effective in terms of quantity or to convey an air of exclusivity with the use of high-quality materials.

In any retail fit-out, a contractor that is a specialist shopfitter will be employed to carry out all of the work on site. Also, in the case of a roll-out, the shopfitter will make the fixtures for every site to the drawings provided by the designer in the design manual. Using one contractor to make all of the fixtures usually cuts costs, as they are then able to create tools to mass-produce all of the internal fixtures.

The main elements of shop display can be examined through three elements: wall fixtures, mid-floor fixtures, and fastenings that complete the functional aspect of the space.

: SARA MANUELLI
British-crafted structures focus on the essence and techniques employed by Mulberry... bespoke leather mannequins, chandeliers and other ephemera aim to challenge the traditional division between shopfitting and art.

Design detail Fixtures and fittings

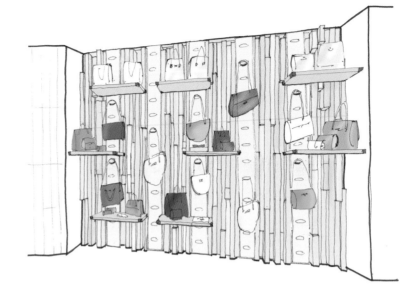

= **MULBERRY**
Concept store

DESIGNER
= **FOUR IV**

DATE
= **2008**

These drawings show the
development of an idea for wall
fixtures for the Mulberry store
concept. The walls are versatile
and can take different formations
of display.

Wall fixtures

The design of the wall fixture is created around the standard size of a panel (1200mm wide x 2400mm high) so it does not have to be jointed, making the fixture more cost-effective and less time consuming to produce. These can be custom made by the shopfitters contracted to fit each site or bought as a kit. The most basic of panels is the slat wall, which is cheap and effective to use. This is a panel that has a series of evenly spaced tracks set within it from which to hang a standard set of hooks, shelves, brackets and rails. These can be bought in different finishes. There are other variations on the slat wall; some contain holes that take hooks, whilst others are planes with just a neutral finish.

A custom-made wall fixture can consist of a number of specialist design features that are unique to the store's scheme, but will always use the standard system of upright posts, hooks, brackets and rails.

When setting out the wall layout, each panel will have what is called a system upright post in between them. These posts have a series of slots that run down them and can hold shelf brackets and clothes rails. It is usual that the wall display will consist of a panel, a shelf at high level for product display and possibly a graphic, and then either a rail for hanging, more shelves evenly spaced, or hooks. It is also possible to connect cabinets to wall displays. These might be used for storage and can commonly be seen in mobile phone stores at the base of each bay; they could also be a glass cabinet for locking away valuable merchandise.

Some wall fixtures are more like pieces of grand furniture than a kit of parts. A men's clothing department displaying shirts and suits may be reminiscent of the design of a Gentleman's club, for instance; and some appear to be built-in, part of the architecture of the interior. In this case the designer is using the building to inform part of the design process, to mix in the architectural detail with the standard scheme, and it is seen more often in one-off stores or small roll-outs.

Design detail Fixtures and fittings

Mid-floor fixtures

There are many variations of mid-floor fixtures that are used for a selection of merchandising purposes. The most common displays are tables at different heights and sizes, gondolas and freestanding cabinets that hold both storage and display. These will sit alongside specialist feature displays, for example, a rack for postcards or a rotating display for CDs.

As well as an interesting display feature, one of the important aspects of the mid-floor fixture is to create merchandising at different levels so that the customer is drawn into the store to view the displays beyond.

The table, often very simply constructed, lends itself to low-level display for smaller items and accessories. Sometimes other merchandising vehicles sit on the tables to prop up merchandise effectively. These are usually clear acrylic stands that are bought from specialist suppliers. Tables are sometimes stacked on top of each other to create more height.

The gondola is an apparatus that works very hard. The design of a gondola can vary in terms of finishes, but almost all are constructed in the same way. It is most commonly used for clothing, but can also be adapted to hold shelves. It is usually designed and constructed using the same materials and fittings as the wall panels. This allows flexibility for the merchandise on display. The gondola is usually designed to be at eye-level height and will consist of a central panel, which sits on a rectangular frame with castors underneath. The panel could be solid or translucent, or simply be a frame, with system upright posts either side. A shelf sits close to the top of the unit for merchandise purposes and in most cases there will be a graphic panel above the shelf. The clothing rails or shelves are supported on brackets from the system upright posts. On both ends of the gondola are opportunities for further display. This would usually be used to tell a story about what is on the gondola – an outfit, for instance.

From store to store, the cabinet is probably the item which changes most significantly in its size, shape and ability to hold stock as it is very dependent on the product. Mobile phone shops and other technological gadgets may be displayed on long, specially designed cabinets with storage underneath; jewellery stores favour timber cabinets with a glass case on top; menswear shops tend to favour cabinets with slots or pigeon holes for ties and shirts, for example.

= MID-FLOOR FIXTURES

This is a mid-floor fixture designed for stacking jeans. Its simple stainless steel construction with timber shelves iis spacious enough to hold a high level of product. The graphic panel on top clearly indicates what's for sale.

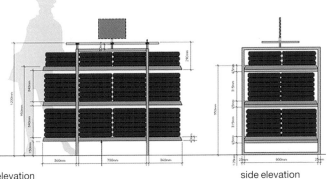

front elevation   side elevation

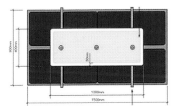

Design detail Fixtures and fittings

Cash desk

One of the most important elements of the interior scheme and one of the hardest to design, is the cash desk. In some cases, the cash desk appears to be no more than a functional piece of furniture, whilst in others the cash desk is the main feature of the space, with branding and a statement wall behind.

The reason that the cash desk is so difficult to design is because it has to contain a lot of equipment. The starting point of designing the cash desk is in understanding exactly what that equipment is, what its function is and the size of each component. Also, the products will demand certain functions from the cash desk. In a clothing store for example, there needs to be space for discarding hangers and in a supermarket there will need to be a conveyor belt.

In its simplest form, the cash desk will need to house a till, which sometimes has a separate register and drawer, a credit card machine, a phone, a drawer for receipt rolls etc., a bin and a space to bag or pack merchandise. The cash desk is most commonly formed from an MDF and soft wood carcass; some have a glass display, whilst others have a more solid panel in the front. The top is often staggered in height so that there is a separate area for staff equipment and a place at a comfortable height to write cheques or use a chip and pin. Also, the desk must have an area that is at a low level for wheelchair users.

Rails, hooks and fastenings

All rails, hooks and fastenings can be bought off the shelf from specialist stockists. They are available in standard sizes and therefore govern the design of all fixtures. It is important for a retail designer to know these standard sizes before designing any form of fixture.

Fixture
The term used to describe specially designed pieces of furniture that hold product and display merchandise.

= **VILLANDRY**
London, UK

DESIGNER
= **DALZIEL AND POW**

DATE
= **2007**

This counter is an important point of sale.
As well as selling and displaying product,
it offers a place to sit. Graphics and
finishes tie in with the rest of the interior.

Design detail Student case study

PROJECT
= **RETAIL SPACE AT THE ISLE OF WIGHT ZOO**

DESIGNER
= **FIONA DAMIANO**

DATE
= **2009**

= The proposed design scheme for the zoo entrance and retail space.

! The Isle of Wight Zoo, situated in Sandown, UK, and constructed within the walls of an existing Victorian fort, is well known for its work, giving sanctuary to tigers, lions, leopards, jaguars, lemurs, monkeys, snakes, spiders and lizards. All of the animals are housed in a wide variety of naturalistic enclosures that encourage them to display their natural behaviours. The zoo's mission is 'to promote the survival of endangered species through first class educational facilities and recreational experiences, exemplary animal management, conservation and research.'

As part of a regeneration programme, a group of students worked directly with the zoo with a view to implementing a new design scheme for the retail and entrance space. As part of the brief, students had to consider the zoo's ethical stance on supporting animal welfare as well as demonstrating sensitivity to material reuse.

This concept by Fiona Damiano combined the precedents of Zaha Hadid's amorphous shapes and Victor Horta's curvilinear whiplash of the art nouveau period, to create a sensual and organic design. The retail space could be accessed by a ramp from the entrance before the journey around the zoo begins, or more commonly entered at the end of the visit, forcing the customer to walk through retail before exiting the whole zoo experience, making a purchase more likely. Fixtures and fittings for product display were positioned in a way specifically to work with the circulation route, and designed intentionally for particular product types. Two separate counters were positioned in strategic places; one at the entrance for ticket sales and a larger one located close to the exit in the retail space. The materials and existing cabinets were reused where possible and were clad and finished in white using the merchandise to add colour and texture.

? Imagine you have designed the concept for a retail interior and are at the detailing and specification stage of the project.

1 What do you want the customer's first impression to be from the street?

2 How can the design of the ceiling and floor become part of the whole scheme and act as a device to sell the brand and enhance the customer experience?

3 What types of wall feature displays could you use that sell the brand?

4 What types of fixtures do you need to enhance the display of products and make them accessible to the customer?

Conclusion

= **LEVI'S FLAGSHIP STORE**
Berlin, Germany

DESIGNER
= **CHECKLAND KINDLEYSIDES**

DATE
= **2008**

This book was compiled as an insightful introduction to designing interior spaces for the retail sector, and to begin to simplify the processes by which the designer approaches this subject area. By unpicking this exciting, fast-moving, creative industry, I hope I have inspired you as new designers in your understanding of what interior design can be as a profession, and how you can see yourself as part of it.

Seeing a design emerge from paper to reality is exciting. It is even more rewarding when people use the space and enjoy the experience in the way in which it was intended. Making spaces happen is a complex art, but can be achieved with creativity, flair and passion.

Next time you enter a store, pause and look around you. Take in the journey that has been painstakingly analysed through market research; what are now age-old principles of retail design and the telling of a story of a brand. Ask yourself, 'What is the message?', 'Why did I choose to enter this store?', 'Why does it appeal to me?' and watch the story unravel. This book will help you to see through what was once in the subconscious and engage with the interior on a different level.

Bibliography

Anderson, J. & Shiers, D. The Green Guide to Specification: Breeam Specification *Wiley Blackwell; 4th Edition*, 2009

Beylerian, G. & Dent, A. Material Connexion: The Global Resource for Innovative Materials for Artists, Architects and Designers *Thames & Hudson, 2005*

Brooker, G. & Stone, S. Rereadings: Interior Architecture and the Design Principles of Remodelling Existing Buildings *RIBA Enterprises, 2004*

de Chatel, F. & Hunt, R. Retailisation: The Here, There and Everywhere of Retail *Europa Publications, 2003*

Conran, T. A Sort of Autobiography Q&A *Harper Collins, 2001*

Curtis, E. Fashion Retail *Wiley-Academy, 2004*

Dean, C. The Inspired Retail Space *Rockport Publishers, 2003*

Din, R. New Retail Conran *Octopus, 2000*

Fitch, R. Fitch on Retail Design *Phaidon Press Limited, 1990*

Fogg, M. Boutique: A 60s Cultural Phenomenon *Mitchell Beazley, 2003*

Giest, J.F. Arcades: The History of a Building Type, *MIT Press, 1983*

Green, W. The Retail Store Design and Construction *iUniverse.com, 1991*

Klein, N. No Logo *Flamingo, 2000*

Lancaster, B. The Department Store: A Social History *Leicester University Press, 1995*

Major, M. & Spe, J. Made of Light, The Art of Light and Architecture *Birkhäuser, 2005*

Manuelli, S. Design for Shopping: New Retail Interiors *Laurence King Publishing, 2006*

Massey, A. Interior Design Since 1900 *Thames and Hudson, 2008*

McDonough, W. & Braungart, M. Cradle to Cradle: Remaking the Way We Make Things *Rodale Press, 2003*

Miller, M. B. The Bon Marché: Bourgeois Culture and the Department Store, 1869–1920 *George Allen & Unwin, 1981*

Moreno S. et al Forefront: The Culture of Shop Window Design *Birkhäuser, 2005*

Mun, D. Shops: A Manual of Planning and Design *The Architectural Press, 1981*

Olins, W. The Brand Handbook *Thames & Hudson, 2008*

Pallasmaa, J. The Eyes of the Skin: Architecture and the Sense *John Wiley & Sons, 2008*

Reis, A. & L. The 22 Immutable Laws of Branding *Harper Collins, 1998*

Riewoldt, Otto Brandscaping: Worlds of Experience in Retail Design *Birkhauser Publishers, 2002*

Scott, K. Shopping Centre Design *Von Nostrand Reinhold Co. Ltd, 1989*

Steel, C. Hungry City: How Food Shapes Our Lives *Chatto & Windus, 2008*

Thorne, R. Covent Garden Market: Its History and Restoration *The Architectural Press, 2008*

Turner, A. W. The Biba Experience *Roger Sears and Isobel Gilan, 2004*

Vernet & de Wit Boutiques and Other Retail Spaces: The Architecture of Seduction *Routledge, 2007*

Yelavich, S. Contemporary World Interiors *Phaidon, 2007*

Zumthor, P. Atmospheres *Birkhäuser, 2006*

Webology

BREEAM: The Building Research Establishment Environmental Assessment Method For Buildings Around the World   www.breeam.org

www.echochamber.com

www.interiordesignhandbook.com

http://materialslibrary.org.uk

www.thecoolhunter.co.uk

Quote sources

014
Knight, P. Nike, *taken from*
De Chatel, F. and Hunt, R.
Retailisation: The Here, There and
Everywhere of Retail
Europa Publications, 2003

016
Olins, W. The Brand Handbook
Thames & Hudson, 2008

019
Reitwoldt, O. Brandscaping:
Worlds of Experience in Retail Design
Birkhäuser, 2002

022
Din, R. New Retail *Conran Octopus, 2000*

024
Caulder Moore Gina *Dubai Press Release,
2008*

038
Thorne, R. Covent Garden Market:
Its History and Restoration
The Architectural Press, 2008

045
Koolhaas, R. *taken from* **De Chatel, F.
and Hunt, R.** Retailisation:
The here, there and everywhere of retail
Europa Publications, 2003

049
Hulanicki, B *taken from* **Fogg, M.**
Boutique: A 60's cultural phenomenon
Mitchell Beazley, 2003

051
Conran, T. A Sort of Autobiography
Q&A, *HarperCollins, 2001*

057
Gardner, J. in *The New York Sun*.
Taken from www.bcj.com *August 2009*

068
Din, R. New Retail *Conran Octopus, 2000*

072
Giest, J.F. Arcades: A History of a Building
Type *MIT Press, 1983*

078
Scott, K Shopping Centre Design
Von Nostrand Reinhold Co. Ltd, 1989

084
Din, R. New Retail *Conran Octopus, 2000*

093
Pallasmaa, J. The Eyes of the Skin:
Architecture and the Sense John
Wiley & Sons, 2008

094
6a Architects *K-Swiss Press Release, 2008*

103
Klein, N. No Logo *Flamingo, 2000*

105
Heap, D. *from* www.danheap.com/
about.html *August 2009*

113
Zumthor, P. Atmospheres *Birkhäuser, 2006*

119
Fitch, R. Fitch on Retail Design
Phaidon Press Limited, 1990

129
Green, W. The Retail Store Design
and Construction *iUniverse.com, 1991*

132
Saguez & Partners Lafayette Maison Press
Release, *2004*

026
Saguez & Partners Lafayette Maison Press
Release, *2004*

142
Wanders, M. *taken from* **Manuelli, S.**
Design for Shopping: New Retail Interiors
Laurence King Publishing, 2006

146
Moreno S. et al Forefront: The Culture
of Shop Window Design *Birkhäuser, 2005*

152
Brooker, G. & Stone, S. Rereadings:
Interior Architecture and the Design
Principles of Remodelling Existing Buildings
RIBA Enterprises, 2004

159
Manuelli, S. Design for Shopping:
New Retail Interiors *Laurence King Publishing,
2006*

Glossary

Acoustics

The word acoustic describes the scientific study of sound. In terms of the interior, sound can be controlled through the use of materials. Hard materials will bounce sound around a space, creating echoes, whilst soft materials will absorb sound, providing a quieter space.

Arcade

An enclosed public shopping area with impressive glass and steel roof structures and ornate decorative facades, that often creates a passageway between high streets.

Atrium

A covered interior space with a glass domed roof, often found in arcades and in the central circulation space of a department store.

Branding

Branding is an approach to marketing products and services under a particular name that has an appeal to a focused group of people. A brand can be a product, a person or a logo. Anything that can be bought and sold as an idea or artefact can be branded.

Brandscaping

This is a term used to describe the mapping of a brand into a three-dimensional space.

Boutique

A small independent fashion retailer, often with a distinct fashion style.

Chain store

The chain store is a design scheme for a retailer that is repeated from city to city.

Circulation

A controlled route one takes around a building.

Concept store

A concept store is a retail space that is used to test and promote new retail schemes for the first time, in a specific location.

Concessions

Concessions are spaces occupied within a department store by key retailers or labels. Concessions are grouped together on each floor depending on the product.

Concourse

The volume of space before or between platforms at train stations and airports.

Consumerism

The purchase of material posessions.

'Cradle to cradle'

This is a term used to describe the constant cyclical reuse of materials: the material is born, used, ripped out and reused.

Department store

A large purpose built building for retail that houses a range of products and labels in the form of concessions.

Facade

The façade is the front elevation of a building. In retailing, the façade acts as an advertisement for the store within, displaying signage and large plate glass windows for display purposes.

Fashion house

A premium fashion label, which has a collection of designers or one key designer working under its name.

Fixture

The term used to describe specially designed pieces of furniture that hold product and display merchandise.

Flagship store

The flagship store is a larger, extended version of a chain store, where a retailer will promote the brand in large prominently positioned sites around the world. It is usually fitted out to a high specification and with unique features that act as a brand statement, and is often exhibition-like in its presentation.

Gondola

A type of fixture that holds hanging garments in a mid-floor position and is usually head height.

Hypermarket

A hypermarket is a larger version of a supermarket, and will often house a generous variety of products that go beyond grocery shopping.

Lifestyle store

A lifestyle store encapsulates a range of products under one venue or brand name, thus giving the consumer the opportunity to buy into a whole lifestyle experience from one retailer.

Lux

The way in which the brightness of light is measured.

Mega centre

A large out of town retail experience that usually combines retail with leisure facilities.

Mood boards

A mood board consists of images taken from books and photographs arranged on a board to describe the feel of the interior space, and the nature of the user.

Pace

Pace describes the speed at which someone moves around the store. Retail designers often consider a range of paces within an interior scheme.

Pop-up store

A pop-up store is a temporary retail environment, that is set up to promote the brand in unusual places, often with an exclusive range of products that are not available in-store or sometimes purely as an interactive advertisement without product.

Product

An object or artefact.

Retail unit

A custom-built space for retail purposes.

Roll-out

This is a term used to describe the reproduction of an interior scheme into a number of different locations. Although the scheme may need to alter to reflect the nature of the site, the principles behind the design idea remain the same.

Shadow gap

A contemporary detail used to create a junction between a wall and a ceiling or floor; or between a fixture and the floor that makes the objects displayed on it appear to be floating.

Sustainability

Using the Earth's natural resources through energy consumption, building and making materials in a way that does not impact on the environment.

System upright posts

Thin, steel posts with a series of slots running up the front face that are used between wall panels to hold rails and shelf brackets.

Virtual shopping

A non-physical retail space accessible online.

Acknowledgements

Creating this book was a challenging and rewarding experience and could not have been achieved without the support and knowledge from AVA Publishers, material provided by leading retail design practices without which the visual content of this book would not have been possible, staff and students from the BA (hons) Interior Design course at the University of Portsmouth's School of Architecture, family and friends.

Therefore, I would like to give special thanks to Leafy Robinson at AVA Publishing for giving me the opportunity to realise this potential and for supporting me throughout the writing process; Keith Ware from Dalziel & Pow, Simon Ash from Brinkworth and Ben Phillips from Shed Design for providing invaluable information and sparing precious time to meet with me; Lorraine Farrelly, Belinda Mitchell and Rachael Brown for your insights and constructive conversations; Terry and June for babysitting when deadlines were tight; and Andrew and Leo for your constant encouragement.

Picture credits

Cover image Frank Oudeman 2010 ©
003 Image provided by Dalziel and Pow.
006 Photograph © James Winspear,
courtesy of Four IV
013 Images provided by Dalziel and Pow
014 Photograph provided by Andrew Mesher
016/017 Images provided by HMKM, London
021 Images provided by Brinkworth
022/023 Images reproduced
courtesy of Shed Design Ltd.
025 Image provided by Caulder Moore
027 Photography courtesy of
Checkland Kindleysides
028 Imagery courtesy of
Checkland Kindleysides
029 Photograph © Richard Davies,
courtesy of John Pawson
030/031 Photography courtesy of
Checkland Kindleysides
032/033 Images provided by
Magdalena Kumala
037 Images courtesy of Shutterstock
039 Image courtesy of Getty
041 Image provided by Dalziel and Pow
043 Photograph © Paul Raftery,
courtesy of View Pictures Ltd
044 Photographs © Yoshiko Seino (Paris),
and Masa Yuki Hayashi (Tokyo),
provided by Amanda Levete Architects
046 Drawing by 6a Architects
047 Photograph by David Grandorge
048/049 Images provided by Dalziel and Pow
051 John Maltby / RIBA Library Photographs
Collection
052/053 Images provided by Droog
054/055 Image provided by Formavision
056 Photo by Ed Uthman
058 Images provided by QuA Associates
060/061 Images provided by
Jekaterina Zlotnikova, Stephanie Harris
and Angeliki Ioannou
065 Photograph © James Winspear,
courtesy of Four IV
066 Photograph by Richard Davies
067 Drawing by Lynne Mesher
070/071 Images provided by Dalziel and Pow
073 Photograph by Lynne Mesher
076 Photographer: Marcin Czajkowski
Courtesy: The Jerde Partnership, Inc.
078 Image courtesy of echochamber.com
080 Images provided by QuA Associates

084/085 Images provided by HMKM, London
088/089 Images provided by Fahirool Adzhar
Muhmad
094 Photographs by David Grandorge
097 Images courtesy of Shutterstock
098 Images courtesy of Shutterstock
099 Images courtesy of Shutterstock
100 Images courtesy of Shutterstock
101 Images courtesy of Shutterstock
102/103 Photography courtesy of
Checkland Kindleysides
104 Photography courtesy of
Checkland Kindleysides
106 Image reproduced courtesy of
Shed Design Ltd.
107 Image provided by Brinkworth
108 Photograph © Rama Knight,
courtesy of Four IV
109 Photograph courtesy of Caulder Moore
110 Drawing by Lynne Mesher
112 Photograph courtesy of Caulder Moore
114/115 Images provided by Caroline Hart
118 Drawing by QuA Associates
122/123 Luc Boegly and Saguez and Partners
124/125 Imagery courtesy of
Checkland Kindleysides
127 Image provided by HMKM, London
129 Drawing by Four IV
131 Image provided by Brinkworth
133 Drawing by QuA Associates
134 Drawing by Lynne Mesher
135 Image provided by Brinkworth
136 Drawing by Lynne Mesher
139 Images provided by Katie Drake-Burrows
144 Drawing by Lynne Mesher
145 Photograph provided by Brinkworth
146 Image provided by Dalziel and Pow
148 Photograph courtesy of Caulder Moore
151 Photography courtesy of
Checkland Kindleysides
153 Images provided by Brinkworth
155 Images reproduced courtesy of
Shed Design Ltd.
157 Images provided by Brinkworth
158 Photograph provided by Amanda Levete
Architects
160 Drawings by Four IV
163 Drawings by Lynne Mesher
165 Image provided by Dalziel and Pow
167 Image provided by Fiona Damiano
168 Photography courtesy of
Checkland Kindleysides

BASICS

INTERIOR DESIGN

Working with ethics

Lynne Elvins
Naomi Goulder

Publisher's note

The subject of ethics is not new, yet its consideration within the applied visual arts is perhaps not as prevalent as it might be. Our aim here is to help a new generation of students, educators and practitioners find a methodology for structuring their thoughts and reflections in this vital area.

AVA Publishing hopes that these **Working with ethics** pages provide a platform for consideration and a flexible method for incorporating ethical concerns in the work of educators, students and professionals. Our approach consists of four parts:

The **introduction** is intended to be an accessible snapshot of the ethical landscape, both in terms of historical development and current dominant themes.

The **framework** positions ethical consideration into four areas and poses questions about the practical implications that might occur. Marking your response to each of these questions on the scale shown will allow your reactions to be further explored by comparison.

The **case study** sets out a real project and then poses some ethical questions for further consideration. This is a focus point for a debate rather than a critical analysis so there are no predetermined right or wrong answers.

A selection of **further reading** for you to consider areas of particular interest in more detail.

Ethical:
aware-
ness/
reflect-
ion/
debate

Introduction

Ethics is a complex subject that interlaces the idea of responsibilities to society with a wide range of considerations relevant to the character and happiness of the individual.

It concerns virtues of compassion, loyalty and strength, but also of confidence, imagination, humour and optimism. As introduced in ancient Greek philosophy, the fundamental ethical question is: *what should I do?* How we might pursue a 'good' life not only raises moral concerns about the effects of our actions on others, but also personal concerns about our own integrity.

In modern times the most important and controversial questions in ethics have been the moral ones. With growing populations and improvements in mobility and communications, it is not surprising that considerations about how to structure our lives together on the planet should come to the forefront. For visual artists and communicators, it should be no surprise that these considerations will enter into the creative process.

Some ethical considerations are already enshrined in government laws and regulations or in professional codes of conduct. For example, plagiarism and breaches of confidentiality can be punishable offences. Legislation in various nations makes it unlawful to exclude people with disabilities from accessing information or spaces. The trade of ivory as a material has been banned in many countries. In these cases, a clear line has been drawn under what is unacceptable.

But most ethical matters remain open to debate, among experts and lay-people alike, and in the end we have to make our own choices on the basis of our own guiding principles or values. Is it more ethical to work for a charity than for a commercial company? Is it unethical to create something that others find ugly or offensive?

Specific questions such as these may lead to other questions that are more abstract. For example, is it only effects on humans (and what they care about) that are important, or might effects on the natural world require attention too?

Is promoting ethical consequences justified even when it requires ethical sacrifices along the way? Must there be a single unifying theory of ethics (such as the Utilitarian thesis that the right course of action is always the one that leads to the greatest happiness of the greatest number), or might there always be many different ethical values that pull a person in various directions?

As we enter into ethical debate and engage with these dilemmas on a personal and professional level, we may change our views or change our view of others. The real test though is whether, as we reflect on these matters, we change the way we act as well as the way we think. Socrates, the 'father' of philosophy, proposed that people will naturally do 'good' if they know what is right. But this point might only lead us to yet another question: *how do we know what is right?*

A framework for ethics

What are your ethical beliefs?

Central to everything you do will be your attitude to people and issues around you. For some people, their ethics are an active part of the decisions they make every day as a consumer, a voter or a working professional. Others may think about ethics very little and yet this does not automatically make them unethical. Personal beliefs, lifestyle, politics, nationality, religion, gender, class or education can all influence your ethical viewpoint.

Using the scale, where would you place yourself? What do you take into account to make your decision? Compare results with your friends or colleagues.

What are your terms?

Working relationships are central to whether ethics can be embedded into a project, and your conduct on a day-to-day basis is a demonstration of your professional ethics. The decision with the biggest impact is whom you choose to work with in the first place. Cigarette companies or arms traders are often-cited examples when talking about where a line might be drawn, but rarely are real situations so extreme. At what point might you turn down a project on ethical grounds and how much does the reality of having to earn a living affect your ability to choose?

Using the scale, where would you place a project? How does this compare to your personal ethical level?

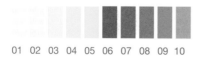

01 02 03 04 05 06 07 08 09 10

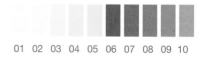

01 02 03 04 05 06 07 08 09 10

YOUR SPECIFICATIONS

What are the impacts of your materials?

In relatively recent times, we are learning that many natural materials are in short supply. At the same time, we are increasingly aware that some man-made materials can have harmful, long-term effects on people or the planet. How much do you know about the materials that you use? Do you know where they come from, how far they travel and under what conditions they are obtained? When your creation is no longer needed, will it be easy and safe to recycle? Will it disappear without a trace? Are these considerations your responsibility or are they out of your hands?

Using the scale, mark how ethical your material choices are.

YOUR CREATION

What is the purpose of your work?

Between you, your colleagues and an agreed brief, what will your creation achieve? What purpose will it have in society and will it make a positive contribution? Should your work result in more than commercial success or industry awards? Might your creation help save lives, educate, protect or inspire? Form and function are two established aspects of judging a creation, but there is little consensus on the obligations of visual artists and communicators toward society, or the role they might have in solving social or environmental problems. If you want recognition for being the creator, how responsible are you for what you create and where might that responsibility end?

Using the scale, mark how ethical the purpose of your work is.

01 02 03 04 05 06 07 08 09 10

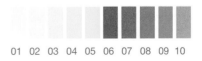

01 02 03 04 05 06 07 08 09 10

The Shakers

One aspect of interior design that raises an ethical dilemma is that of creating interior spaces that may directly affect people's health and well-being. For example, some studies have found concentrations of VOCs (volatile organic compounds) up to ten times higher indoors than outdoors. VOCs are emitted, amongst other things, by paints, lacquers, flooring materials and furnishings.
The adverse health effects of over exposure to harmful VOCs can include eye and throat irritation, headaches, fatigue, dizziness and nausea. Electrical fields generated by everyday equipment, such as computers, and excess static electricity created by certain materials, could also be bad for human health. Prolonged exposure to electrical fields may cause increased risk of respiratory diseases and infection, airborne bacteria and viruses. At what point should (or do) interior design projects take into account these and other health issues? Is it the responsibility of the interior designer to consider potential risks based on inconclusive evidence that is still being explored and debated? Or is it the responsibility of scientific researchers and governments working with the manufacturers of the materials under question?

The Shakers were a religious sect that went to America from England in 1774 seeking freedom from religious persecution. They pursued complete independence from 'the outside world', which led them to build their own properties and design their own objects.

Shaker interiors were entirely free of ornament, contrasting starkly with the mainstream excesses of the Victorian appetite for the fancy and elaborate. Beadings or mouldings were stripped away. Walls were plain white and painted floors were kept bare for easy cleaning. On entering a Shaker building, one commentator wrote: 'The first impression of all is cleanliness, with a suggestion of bareness which is not inconsistent, however, with comfort, and which comes chiefly from the aspect of unpapered walls, the scrubbed floors hidden only by rugs and strips of carpeting, and the plain flat finish of the woodwork.'

Window frames, chimneys and stairways were all executed with clean lines in basic forms. The results reflected total simplicity, remarkable functionality and beautifully proportioned craftsmanship. Shakers designed everything with careful thought, working with the belief that to produce something well was in itself 'an act of prayer'.

Shakers lived communal lives, so furniture was built and arranged for efficient use by large numbers of people. Everything was functional, including chairs, benches, tables and huge banks of storage cabinets with drawers. Lines of wooden pegs around a room were used to hang up chairs, baskets and hats. Furniture was made out of pine or other inexpensive wood, and so was light in colour and weight. The interior of Shaker meeting houses included large, open floor space to allow for their religious dances. The important factors within any building were considered to be the quality of light, an equal distribution of heat, general care for protection and comfort, and other factors that pertained to health and long life. Typical communal bedrooms might contain simple rope beds, washbasins and wood-burning stoves. Storage boxes, clocks, brooms and woven materials were also created, with some products made available to sell.

By the middle of the twentieth century, collectors, inspired by the modernist assertion that 'form follows function', were drawn to Shaker artefacts at the same time as Shaker communities were themselves disappearing. Original Shaker furniture is costly and still sought after today, due to its quality and historical significance.

If an interior design is inspired by religious belief, does it make the result more ethical?

How might decoration seem more unethical than plainness?

Would you work on providing a Shaker interior to a wealthy private client?

WILLIAM MORRIS
Ornamental pattern work, to be raised above the contempt of reasonable men, must possess three qualities: beauty, imagination and order.

AIGA
Design Business and Ethics
2007, AIGA

Eaton, Marcia Muelder
Aesthetics and the Good Life
1989, Associated University Press

Ellison, David
Ethics and Aesthetics in European Modernist Literature:
From the Sublime to the Uncanny
2001, Cambridge University Press

Fenner, David E W (Ed)
Ethics and the Arts:
An Anthology
1995, Garland Reference Library of Social Science

Gini, Al and Marcoux, Alexei M
Case Studies in Business Ethics
2005, Prentice Hall

McDonough, William and Braungart, Michael
Cradle to Cradle:
Remaking the Way We Make Things
2002, North Point Press

Papanek, Victor
Design for the Real World:
Making to Measure
1972, Thames & Hudson

United Nations Global Compact
The Ten Principles
www.unglobalcompact.org/About TheGC/TheTenPrinciples/index.html